Fabric Lovers'
Christmas Scrapcrafts

Fabric Lovers' Christmas Scrapcrafts

Dawn Cusick

A Sterling/Lark Book
Sterling Publishing Co., Inc.   New York

Photography: Evan Bracken, Light Reflections
Design: Kathleen Holmes
Production: Elaine Thompson, Kathleen Holmes
Illustrations: Kathleen Holmes

Library of Congress Cataloging-in-Publication Data
Cusick, Dawn.
    Fabric lovers' Christmas scrapcrafts / Dawn Cusick.
    "A Sterling/Lark book."
    Includes bibliographical references and index.
    ISBN 0-8069-0437-2
    1. Christmas decorations.   2. Textile crafts.   I. Title
TT900-C4C85   1993
745.594'12--dc20

                                        93-10659
                                        CIP

10 9 8 7 6 5 4 3 2 1

A Sterling/Lark Book

Produced by Altamont Press, Inc.
  50 College Street, Asheville, NC 28801 USA

Published in 1993 by Sterling Publishing Co., Inc.
  387 Park Avenue South, New York, NY 10016 USA

Copyright © 1993, Altamont Press

Distributed in Canada by Sterling Publishing
  c/o Canadian Manda Group, P.O. Box 920, Station U
  Toronto, Ontario, Canada M8Z 5P9
Distributed in the United Kingdom by Cassell PLC
  Villiers House, 41/47 Strand, London WC2N 5JE, England
Distributed in Australia by Capricorn Link Ltd.,
  P.O. Box 665, Lane Cove, NSW 2066

Printed in Hong Kong by Mandarin Printing

ISBN 0-8069-0437-2

Contents

Introduction 8

Materials and Tips 9

Gift Traditions 10

Endearing Miniatures 28

Kitchen Inspirations 36

Yuletide Whimsies 46

Culinary Celebrations 64

Santa's Treasures....................76

Irresistible Patchwork 94

Victorian Enchantments......106

Delectable Confections 116

Bibliography and Index 128

See project instruction on page 126.

Introduction

Welcome to Fabric Lovers' Christmas Scrapcrafts. Hopefully, it will only take a few minutes of browsing before you'll be bursting with ideas. As you look through the projects, don't be afraid to mix and match ideas from different chapters or to substitute different fabrics and notions. Innovation and adaptation are a scrapcrafter's best tools.

Here's your chance to use up all those scraps you've been saving because you just knew they had the potential to become something special. And, since many of the projects require only small pieces, now's the time to experiment with expensive fabrics such as brocades and silks. As you'll see, some of the projects in this book can be completed in just a few minutes and will adorn your home for several holidays, while others will take much longer to make but will be cherished by generations to come.

My own introduction to scrapcrafting came as a teenager, when my mother devised the following incentive to keep me busy (and out of trouble): There would be no more clothes-buying excursions to the local department store, but I could have all the clothes I could make from her large inventory of cloth. Knowing how teenagers covet clothes, you can imagine the glee (and greed) I felt as I rummaged through her fabrics. Soon, though,

I realized the true challenge behind her offer. My mother was (and still is) an absolute genius at finding beautiful remnants at great prices. The problem with these remnants, though, was that there was rarely anything large enough to make an entire outfit. Thus, all my clothing for the next few years had yokes, collars, and pockets in contrasting fabrics. It was frustrating at first, but the results blessed me with the incomparable pleasure that comes from making something special from virtually nothing.

Watching the projects in this book evolve from just a glimmer of an idea to a fully completed fabric decoration elicited similar thrills, and I hope you'll enjoy the same feeling as you finish each project. A special thanks goes out to all the designers who contributed their work to this book, and to the people who allowed us to use their homes and businesses for photography.

See project instructions on page 127.

Success Tips

🦌 Choose fabrics and notions that give you a thrill. Don't just go looking for a scrap of red or green holiday print fabric — keep searching until you find one that makes your heart skip a beat. Look for notions like ribbons and buttons whose sparkle fills you with holiday spirit every time you look at them.

🦌 Don't judge a project when it's half finished. Lots of potentially beautiful projects end up in the garbage because someone's having a bad day or not able to envision the finished project. If you still don't care for the project when it's finished, consider adding some glitz with some metallic thread, fabric paint, or other festive notion.

🦌 Although this sounds like a silly suggestion, spend 20 minutes or so reading the backs of the glue bottles in your nearest craft store. If you haven't done this recently, you'll be amazed at the new varieties and abilities. There are glues for bonding metals, glues for fabrics, and glues billing themselves as all-purpose craft glues. Glue guns are also an option for fabric crafters, although the small working areas may make the new low-melt glue guns a better choice. Whenever you're working with craft or fabric glues, always allow enough time for the glue to dry completely before you handle the project.

🦌 No matter how excited you are to get started right away, be sure to wash your fabrics before working with them to prevent shrinkage and bleeding problems.

🦌 Consider using iron-on adhesive webbing instead of traditional appliqué methods to attach fabrics. This relatively new product is sold under a variety of trade names. On one side the webbing resembles a heavy interfacing fabric; on the other side, the webbing is coated with a type of paper that releases an even layer of glue when exposed to the heat of an iron. Be sure to follow the specific manufacturer instructions that come with the product.

🦌 Please note that many of the quilting projects assume a knowledge of basic quilting. If you don't feel comfortable with a technique, such as mitering, for instance, take a brief look at a well-illustrated quilting book and you shouldn't have any problems.

See project instructions on page 127.

Gift Traditions

Decorating the Christmas tree with handmade ornaments is perhaps the most satisfying part of the holidays for scrapcrafters. Every step along the way, from choosing and sewing the fabrics to finding just the right branch to showcase the ornament, seems to have a magical way of embodying the maker with that ever-elusive feeling known as "The Christmas Spirit." Even holiday retailers have come to recognize the Christmas tree as a special place for self revelation, and are marketing ornaments designed to symbolize lifetime events and celebrate special hobbies.

The ornaments in this chapter require just small scraps of fabric and a few minutes of your time. The velvet poinsettias are a little more complicated, but they can be displayed between the branches of your tree or arranged in a clay pot. The poinsettia pattern can also be reduced by 50% to make smaller poinsettias for package decorations or hair ornaments. The quilted pouch ornaments can be hung on the tree as they are or filled with ornaments, chocolates, or small gifts. The scrapcraft clothing projects make wonderful gifts, although you may become so attached to them during the making that you won't want to give them away.

Velvet Poinsettias

Materials

Scraps of red velvet
Scraps of red cotton
Scraps of green velvet
Dark red thread
Gold balls, 1/2 inch (13 mm) in diameter
3/8-inch (10 mm) wooden dowel rods, cut into
    3-inch (7-1/2 cm) lengths
Green acrylic paint
Floral wire

Instructions

🦌 Paint the dowels green and allow them to dry while you're constructing the poinsettia leaves. Cut 15 petals from the red velvet, 15 from the red cotton, and six from the green velvet. With right sides together, sew the red velvet and red cotton petals together, leaving the bottom open. Turn right sides out. Zigzag the veins and stitch the bottom ends closed. Do the same for all the petals, including the green velvet leaves.

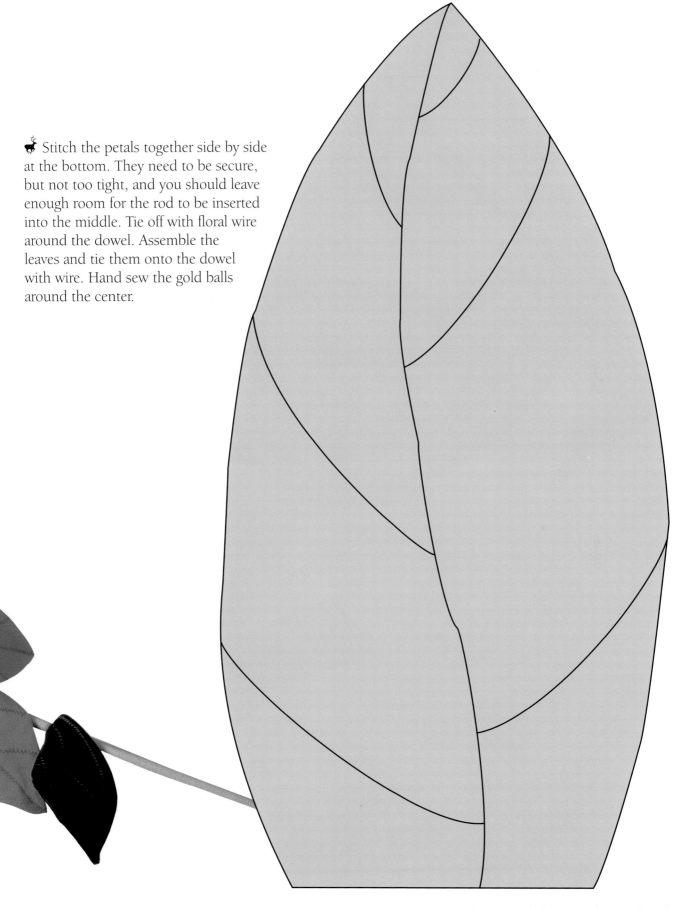

Stitch the petals together side by side at the bottom. They need to be secure, but not too tight, and you should leave enough room for the rod to be inserted into the middle. Tie off with floral wire around the dowel. Assemble the leaves and tie them onto the dowel with wire. Hand sew the gold balls around the center.

Patchwork Hanging Pouches

Materials

Fabric scraps
Plaid ribbon
Red ribbon roses
Quilt batting
Glue gun
Red shoelaces

Instructions

Cut out the four sides of the pouch. Sew the scraps into half round blocks or in a random pattern. Sew the batting to the wrong side of the quilted fabric, and then sew the front and back sides with the wrong sides together. Turn inside out and slip stitch. Repeat the process for the back, using plain fabric instead of patchwork if desired.

With right sides together, stitch the front and back of the pouch, leaving an opening on the top of the pouch. Attach the shoelaces on both sides with hot glue. Tie the ribbon into two bows and attach each bow to one side of the pouch with hot glue. Arrange the roses on the front of the pouch and hot-glue them in place.

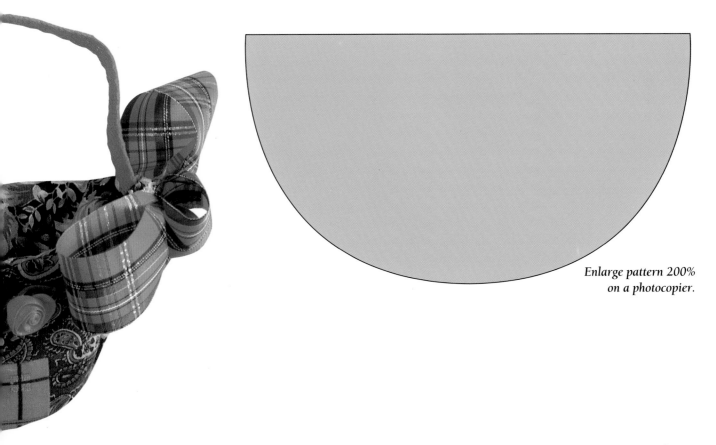

*Enlarge pattern 200%
on a photocopier.*

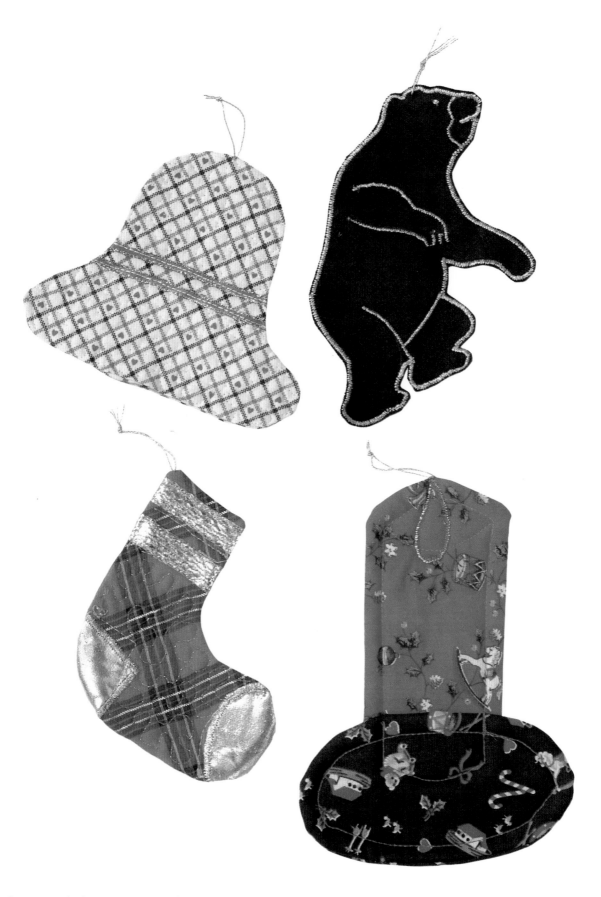

Bell Ornament

Materials for Each Ornament

Scraps of several holiday fabrics
Scraps of batting
Scraps of gold braid
Gold metallic thread

Instructions

🦌 With right sides together, cut out two bell patterns from the fabric and one from the batting. Sew the braid on the right side of each pattern piece. Position the two fabric bells on top of each other with their right sides together, and then place the batting on the top bell. Stitch around the sides, leaving the bottom open. Clip the curves and turn. Press well. Hand stitch the bottom opening closed and then quilt as desired. Last, make a hanging loop from the gold thread and attach it to the ornament with a needle.

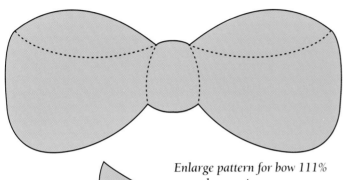

Enlarge pattern for bow 111% on a photocopier.

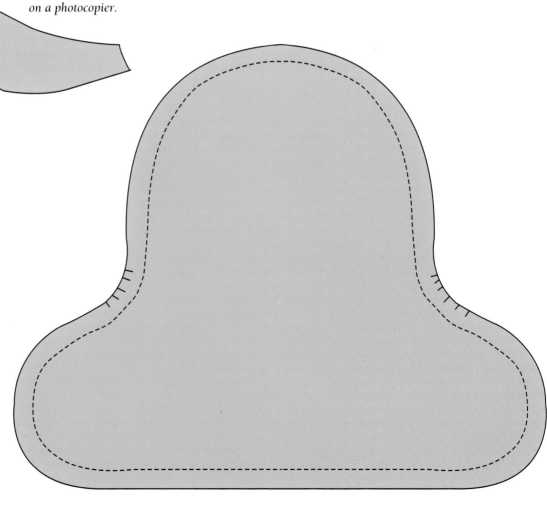

Stocking Ornament

Materials for Each Ornament

Scraps of plaid fabric
Scraps of batting
Scraps of gold lamé
Scraps of gold braid
Gold metallic thread
Iron-on webbing

Instructions

🦌 With right sides together, cut out the stocking pattern from the fabric and then from the batting. Press the iron-on webbing to the back side of the gold lamé, and then cut out two toe and two heel pieces for the lamé. Peel off the paper after it cools and then position the heel and toe pieces on the right sides of both stockings. Sew the edges of the lamé with a small appliqué stitch using the gold metallic thread.

🦌 Sew the braid across the top of each stocking piece. Position the two fabric stockings on top of each other with their right sides together, and then place the batting on the top stocking. Sew around the edges, leaving a small opening as indicated on the pattern. Clip the curves, turn right sides out, and press well. Quilt as desired, and then make a hanging loop from the gold thread and attach it to the ornament with a needle.

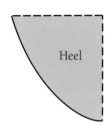

Heel

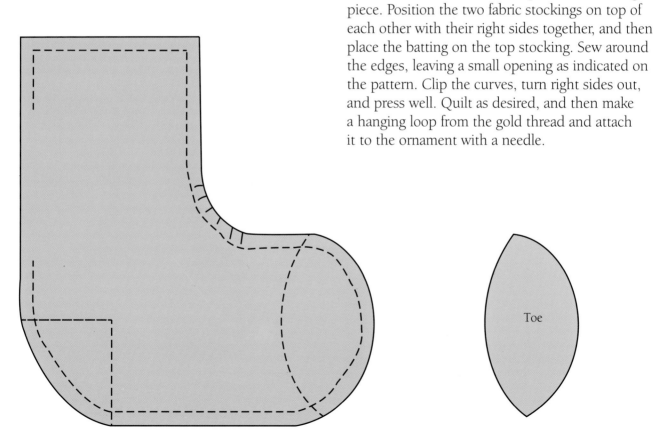

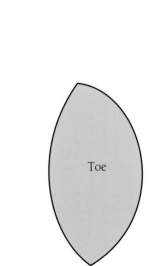

Toe

Candle Ornament

Materials for Each Ornament

Scraps of two contrasting fabrics for candle and base
Scraps of batting
Scraps of gold lamé for the flame
Iron-on webbing
Gold metallic thread

Instructions

🦌 Cut out two candles and two bases from the fabrics, and then cut out one candle and one base from the batting. Position the two candle pieces on top of each other with their right sides together, and then place the batting on the top candle piece. Sew the three layers together, leaving a small opening as indicated on the pattern. Clip the curves, turn right sides out, and press well. Repeat the process for the base. Sew all of the sides closed and then make a slit on the back side as indicated on the pattern. Turn the base right sides out through the slit and press well.

🦌 Next, hand or machine quilt the candle and base pieces. Press the iron-on webbing to the back side of the gold lamé, and then cut out flame. Peel off the paper after it cools and then position the flame on top of the candle and iron in place. Top stitch the candle to the base. Last, make a hanging loop from the gold thread and attach it to the ornament with a needle.

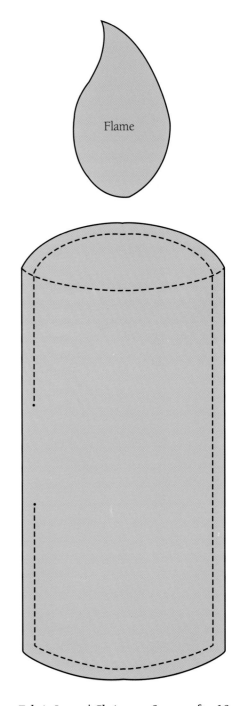

Flame

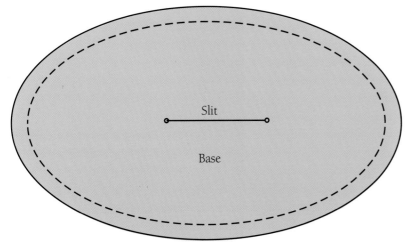

Slit

Base

Candy Cane Ornament

Materials for Each Ornament

Scraps of red and white striped fabric
Scraps of stuffing material
Gold metallic thread

Instructions

♣ With right sides together, cut out the candy cane pattern. Stitch the two pieces together with their right sides facing, leaving a small opening as indicated on the pattern. Clip the curves, turn right sides out, and stuff until very full. Hand stitch the opening closed. Last, make a hanging loop from the gold thread and attach it to the ornament with a needle.

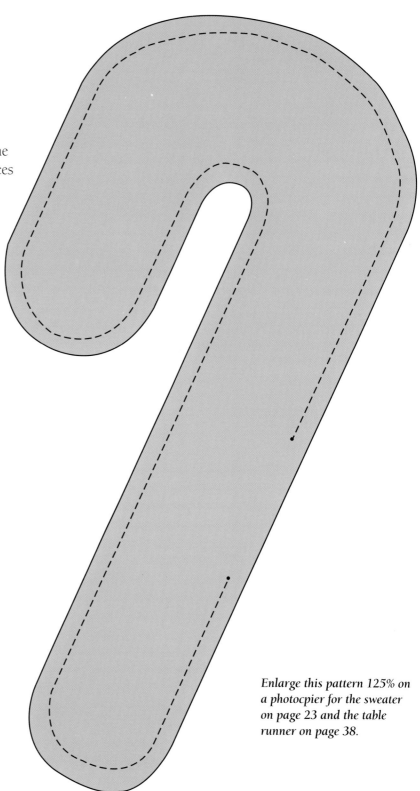

Enlarge this pattern 125% on a photocpier for the sweater on page 23 and the table runner on page 38.

A custom valance that matches the fabric ornaments is simple and fun to make. Start by appliqueing the shapes to rectangles of fabric. Border the rectangles and sew them together. For a good fit, the finished valance should be 9 inches (22 cm) longer than your rod. Finish the valance as you would a place mat or full size quilt. Last, make the valance's casing by pressing a long, narrow strip of fabric down on all four sides down 1/2 inch (13 mm) and then sewing it across the top of the valance on the back side.

Bear Ornament

Materials for Each Ornament

2 scraps of polished black cotton measuring at least
    6 x 4 inches (15 x 10 cm)
Iron-on webbing
Small piece of mylar
Chalk pencil
Gold metallic thread

Instructions

🦌 Iron a piece of iron-on webbing to the wrong side of a piece of the black fabric. Allow it to cool and then remove the paper. Place the two pieces of black fabric together with their wrong sides facing each other and press well to release the webbing's adhesive.

🦌 Place the mylar over the bear pattern and cut it out. Then position the pattern on the fabric and trace the bear's outlines with the chalk pencil. Do not cut out the fabric yet. Sew over the tracing with a narrow appliqué stitch in gold metallic thread. Last, make a hanging loop from the gold thread and attach it to the ornament with a needle.

Christmas Sweater

Materials

Oversized red cardigan sweater or jacket
Iron-on webbing
Green and brown velvet scraps
Ribbon scraps
Charms, sequins, beads, trims, and other notions
that catch your fancy

Approximately 1/2 yard (.5 m) of red and white
striped fabric
Fringe tassel trim
Red velvet ribbon
Quilt batting scraps

Instructions

🦌 Cut out the Christmas tree, packages, and candy canes shapes. (Enlarge the candy cane pattern on page 20 by 125%. Form the packages by cutting rectangles out of fabric.) Cut out a piece of quilt batting and a piece of iron-on webbing for each of the shapes. Sew the quilt batting onto the wrong side of each shape.

🦌 Iron the webbing onto the wrong side of the Christmas tree. Position the tree in the center back of the sweater and iron in place. Repeat the process with the candy canes, positioning one on each shoulder. Decorate the packages with scraps of ribbon and then iron the webbing to their wrong sides. Position some of the packages under the tree and the remainder on the front of the sweater, and iron them in place. Using contrasting thread colors, zig-zag the edges of all of the motifs.

🦌 Decorate the tree and the packages with an assortment of beads, sequins, ribbons, buttons, charms, and other trims. The sequins can be positioned next to each other to create a tree garland. Finish by attaching the fringe down the front sides and around the neck.

Enlarge the pattern 200% on a photocopier.

Holiday Sweatshirts

Materials

Sweatshirts
Iron-on webbing
Holiday print fabric with large motifs
Craft jewels
Craft glue
Assorted fabric paints (Opalescent white, green,
glitter gold, and glitter green were used in
the shirts shown here.)

Instructions

🦌 Cut out the fabric motifs you plan to use. Use the motifs as a pattern to cut out backings of iron-on webbing. Attach the webbing to the back of the motifs with an iron. Position the motifs to form a pleasing design and then iron them in place.

🦌 Outline the motifs with fabric paint and embellish as desired with craft jewels. For a glowing effect as seen in the poinsettia leaves, outline the shape with gold glitter paint and then use a pencil tip to pull some of the paint outward.

Endearing Miniatures

*H*oliday retailers seem to have *finally realized that large Christmas trees do not meet the lifestyle needs and desires of many of their customers, and they're even making lovely collections of miniature ornaments and garlands to decorate smaller trees. It's difficult to resist the intrinsic charm and space-saving size of these small trees, and even if you have room for a large tree, you may find that placing a little tree in a guest or child's room makes everyone in your home feel more involved in the holiday season.*

Designed to be functional as well as decorative, the tree skirt features pouches that can be filled with small gifts or decorations. The fabric packages look wonderful protruding slightly from the pouches, or they can be used as ornaments for a larger tree. The small fabric mice scampering around the base of the tree have been filled with allspice berries and crushed cinnamon sticks to fill the air with Christmas fragrance. This ensemble makes the perfect gift for someone in a nursing home or hospital.

Miniature Tree Skirt

Materials

2 yards (1.8 m) of red calico
2 yards of green calico
Chalk
Fabric scraps
Red eyelet
Red satin roses
Glue gun
Quilt batting

Instructions

🦌 Place the red calico face down on top of the table on which you plan to display the tree and trace the shape onto the fabric with the chalk. Add a 5/8-inch (15 mm) seam allowance and cut out. Use this circle as a pattern to cut out the green calico and a piece of batting. Stitch the batting to the wrong side of one of the circles.

🦌 Measure the distance around the outside of the circle. Then cut a length of 6-inch (14 cm) wide fabric that's twice the length of the distance around the circle. With wrong sides together, fold the fabric in half lengthwise and press. Add a row of gathering stitches along the unfinished edges and gather until the ruffle fits the circle. Baste the ruffle to the right side of one of the circles. Place the circles right sides together and stitch most of the way around, leaving an opening large enough for turning. Turn the circles right sides out, slip stitch the opening closed, and press.

🦌 With right sides together, stitch the front and back sides of the each pouch together, leaving an opening on the top of the pouch. Turn the pouches right side out, press, and slip stitch the openings closed. Arrange the pouches around the tree skirt and stitch them in place. Add trims such as eyelet and satin roses with hot glue.

Enlarge pattern 125% on a photocopier for the smaller pouches and 150% for the larger pouches.

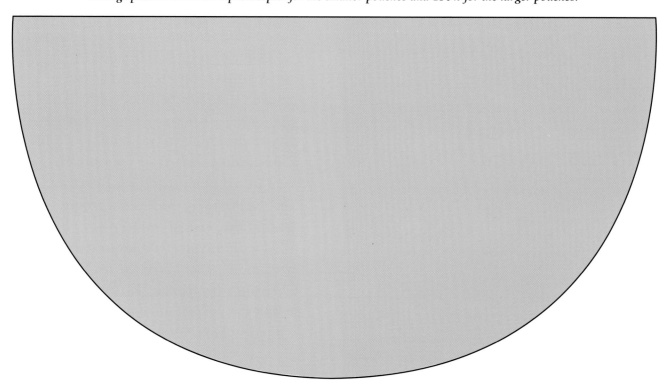

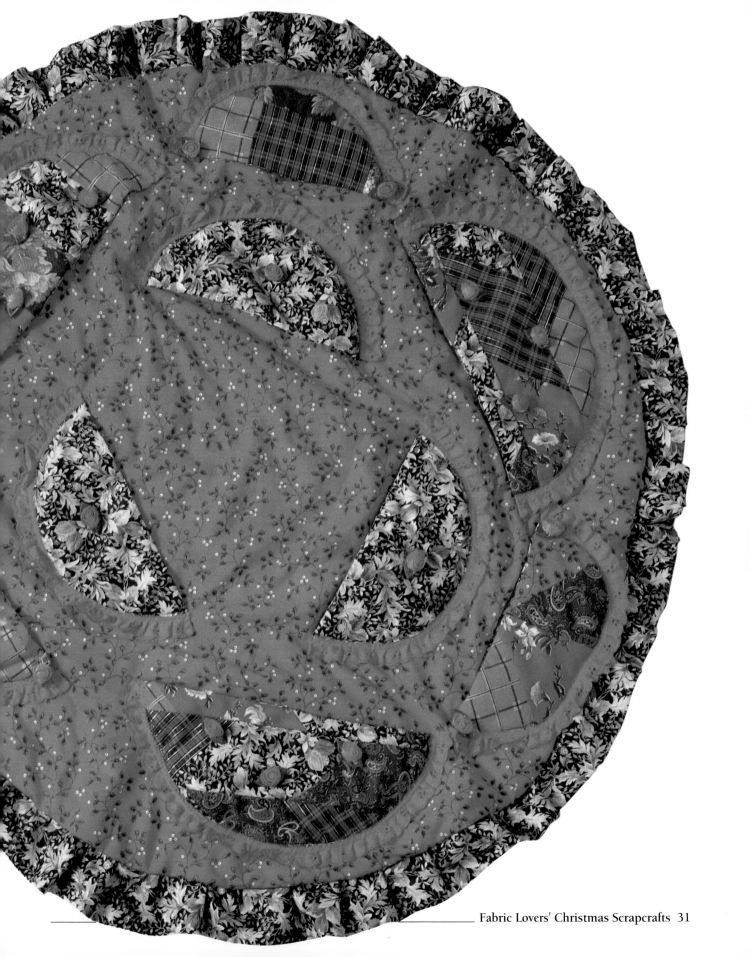

Patchwork Package Ornaments

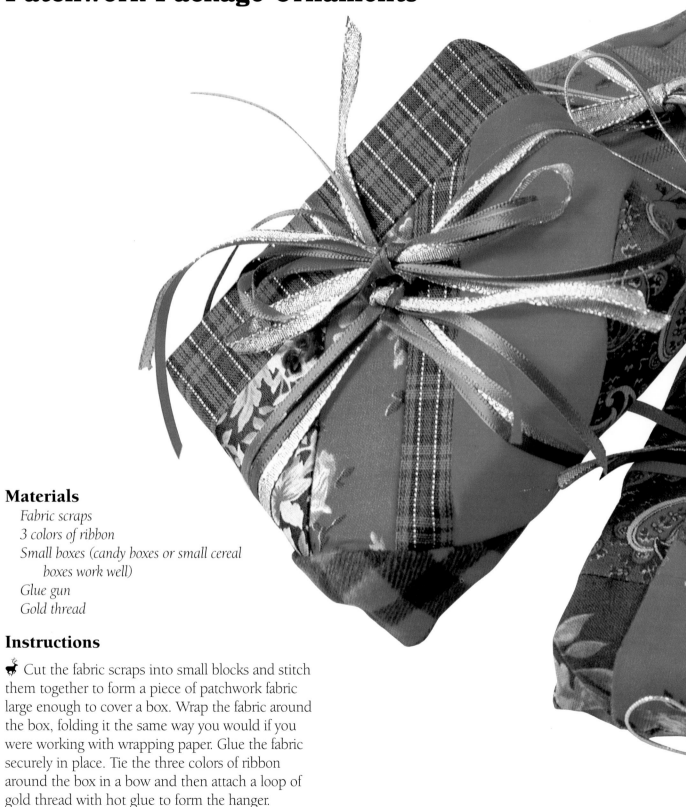

Materials

Fabric scraps
3 colors of ribbon
Small boxes (candy boxes or small cereal
   boxes work well)
Glue gun
Gold thread

Instructions

🦌 Cut the fabric scraps into small blocks and stitch them together to form a piece of patchwork fabric large enough to cover a box. Wrap the fabric around the box, folding it the same way you would if you were working with wrapping paper. Glue the fabric securely in place. Tie the three colors of ribbon around the box in a bow and then attach a loop of gold thread with hot glue to form the hanger.

Potpourri Mice

Materials for Each Mouse

Cotton fabric scraps
Felt scraps
3 small beads
Potpourri
Cotton ball

Instructions

🦌 Cut out the mouse's body from the cotton fabric. Cut two small circles about the size of a quarter and a long, narrow tail from the felt. Machine or hand sew the top two body pieces together and press. Then sew the top and bottom together about three-fourths of the way.

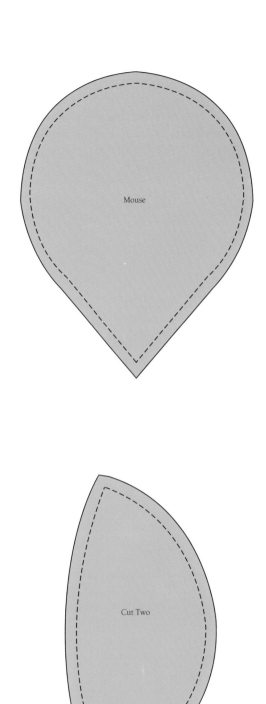

Mouse

Cut Two

🦌 Stuff the mouse with potpourri and cotton, and then hand stitch the opening shut. Stitch or glue the ears, eyes, and tail in place. Last, form the whiskers by threading needle with heavy thread and running it through the fabric above the mouse's nose. Cut the thread at the desired length and repeat two more times for a total of three whiskers.

Kitchen Inspirations

The kitchen is a popular gathering place during the holiday season, perhaps because the wonderful smells of holiday goodies emanating from the oven prove an irresistible lure to anyone in the vicinity. The sewing projects in this room are both functional and decorative, making them all the more treasured. The candy cane table runner and chair pads can be easily custom-fit to your kitchen furniture. The runner features a large center bow and stuffed candy canes at both ends. If you remove the candy canes, the runner can be used a few months later as a decoration to celebrate Valentine's Day.

The scrap fabric wreaths can be made with a large base and then displayed as a traditional wall wreath, or made from a much smaller base and displayed with a candle in the middle for a table centerpiece. (If you'd like to display the wreath outdoors, just spray it with a substantial layer of fabric stiffener.) The little girl's appliquéd and quilted dress is made from plaids and solids in holiday colors (instead of a Santa Claus print), so that it looks festive during the holiday season yet makes the transition to year 'round clothing with ease.

Candy Cane Table Runner

Materials

*Wide-striped red and white fabric (approximately
    3 yards, 2.7 m)*
Scraps of narrow-striped red and white fabric
Polyester quilt batting
Fabric glue (optional)
Heavy gold thread

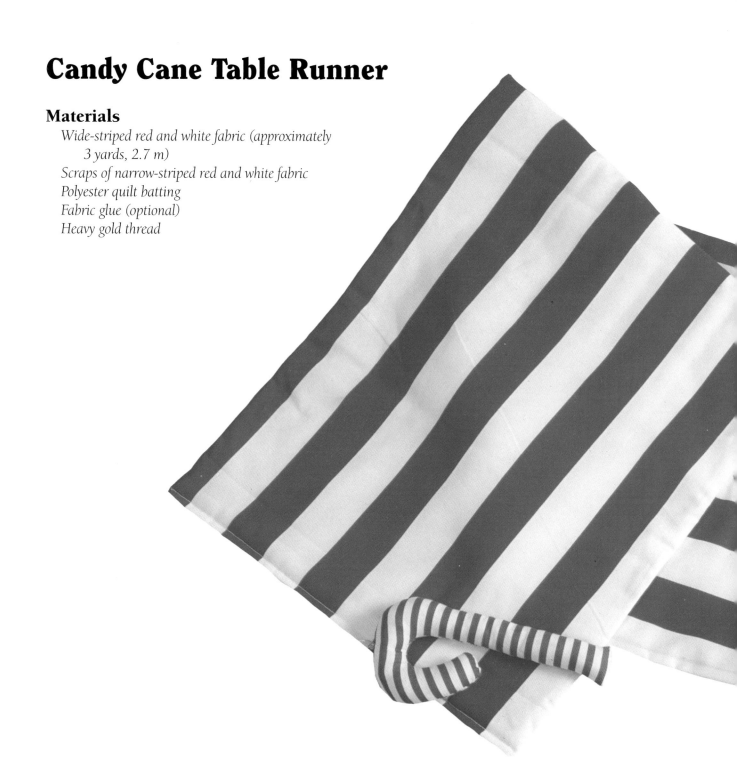

Instructions

🦌 Cut two pieces of the wide-striped fabric long enough to drape over the edges of the table and wide enough to complement the width of your table top. Cut a piece of batting to match. (Enlarge the pattern on page 20 by 125%.) With the pattern positioned on the fold, cut out two candy cane shapes from the narrow-striped fabric. Last, cut out a 1-yard x 6-inch (.9 m x 15 cm) length of wide-striped fabric and tie it in a bow.

🦌 Position the bow in the center of one of the table runner fabric lengths and secure it in place with a zig-zag stitch. Next, fit the batting to one piece of the table runner and stitch it to the wrong side. Place the right sides of the table runner pieces together and stitch them together, leaving a small opening for turning. Turn the runner right sides out and glue or slip stitch the opening closed.

🦌 With right sides facing, stitch the candy canes together, leaving a small opening for turning. Turn the candy canes right sides out, fill them with stuffing, and glue or slip stitch the opening closed. Hang one candy cane from each end of the runner with gold thread.

Candy Cane Chair Cushions

Materials

Wide-striped red and white fabric (approximately
 3 yards, 2.7 m, per chair)
Scraps of narrow-striped red and white fabric
Polyester batting
Fabric glue (optional)
Durable, colorful ribbon, 1 inch wide (2-1/2 cm)

Instructions

🦌 Place a piece of newspaper or tissue paper over the seat area of your chair and trace the shape to form a pattern. Add a seam allowance to all sides of the shape and cut it out. For each chair, cut out two pieces of the wide-striped fabric and one piece of batting. Sew the batting to the wrong side of one of the fabric pieces.

🦌 Measure the distance around the front and sides of your chair cushion, and cut a strip of fabric that is 6 inches (15 cm) wide and double the distance you measured in length. Fold the fabric in half lengthwise, right sides together, to form a tube. Sew the long seam, turn the tube right sides out, and press. Gather the ruffle to match the size of the front and sides of the cushion. Place the two cushion pieces right sides together and pin the ruffle inside to the front and sides. Stitch the cushion together, leaving an opening on the back side large enough for turning. Turn the cushion right sides out and glue or slip stitch the opening closed.

🦌 To make the bows, cut two 4- x 24-inch (10 x 61 cm) lengths of the wide-striped fabric. Fold each one in half lengthwise and stitch the long seam. Turn the tubes right sides out and press. Glue or slip stitch the openings closed. Tie each tube in a bow and embellish with a scrap of narrow-striped red and white fabric tied around the center. Pin or stitch the bows to the back sides of the chair pads. Last, attach a length of ribbon to the underside of the cushion to tie around the chair's spindles.

Scrap Fabric Wreaths

Materials

*Several colors of 3-1/2- x 3-1/2-inch (8 x 8 cm)
    fabric squares (approximately 3 yards,
    2.7 m, of assorted scraps for a large wreath,
    or 3/4 yard, .6 m, for a small wreath)*
*Straw wreath base covered with green plastic
    or plastic kitchen wrap*
Screwdriver
Ribbons

Instructions

🦌 Use the screwdriver to poke a hole in the wreath
base. Then gather up a fabric square from its center
back and push it into the hole. Continue adding
fabric scraps in this way until the wreath is covered, paying attention to creating a lush look without space gaps. Finish by poking in loops of contrasting ribbon.

Appliquéd and Quilted Dress

Materials

Purchased jumper pattern that has a lined top
Fabrics as called for in your pattern instructions
1/4 yard (.2 m) fleece
Scraps of contrasting fabric for appliqué
Iron-on webbing
Freezer paper

Instructions

🦌 Cut out the jumper as directed in the purchased pattern instructions. Cut out a piece of fleece using the top back and top front pattern. Baste the fleece to the wrong side of top front and top back fabrics, and then assemble the top portion of the dress as directed. Press well. Machine or hand quilt the top of the dress in the pattern of your choice.

🦌 Cut out one each of the rose and leaf appliqué in the fabric and the iron-on webbing. Attach the webbing to the back of the rose and leaves, following the manufacturer's instructions. Arrange the motifs on the front of the jumper and iron them in place.

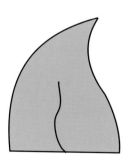

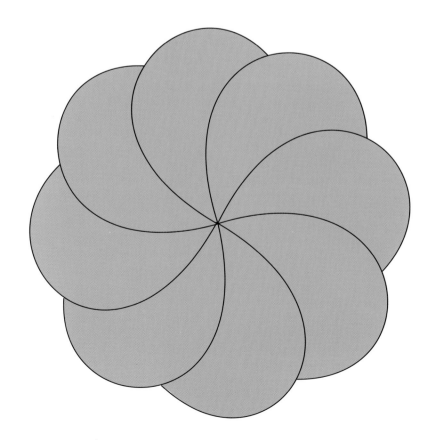

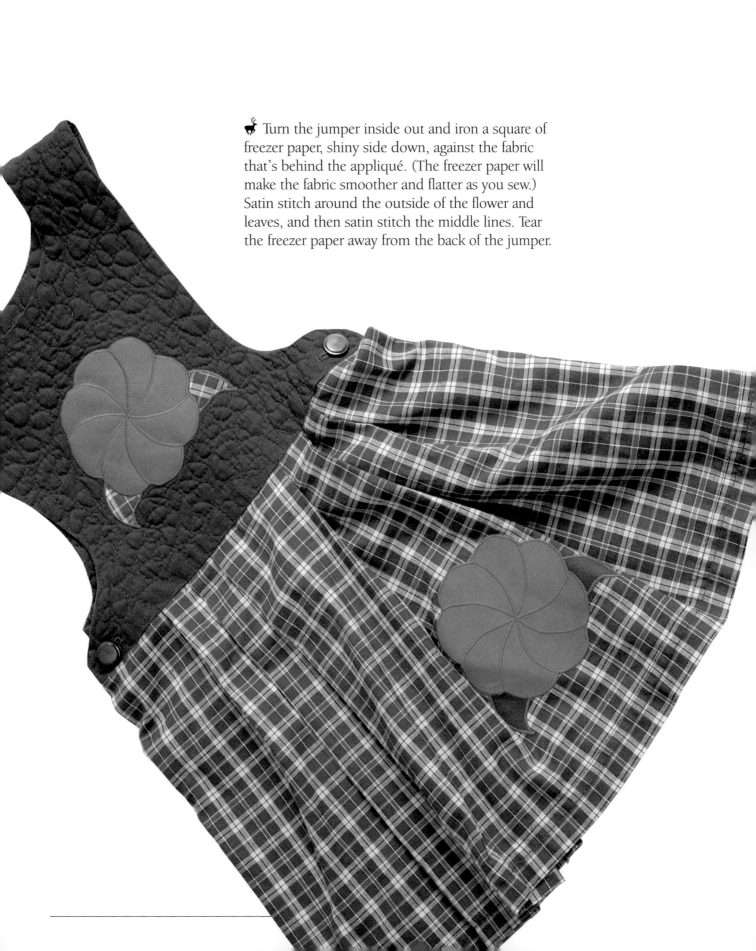

Turn the jumper inside out and iron a square of freezer paper, shiny side down, against the fabric that's behind the appliqué. (The freezer paper will make the fabric smoother and flatter as you sew.) Satin stitch around the outside of the flower and leaves, and then satin stitch the middle lines. Tear the freezer paper away from the back of the jumper.

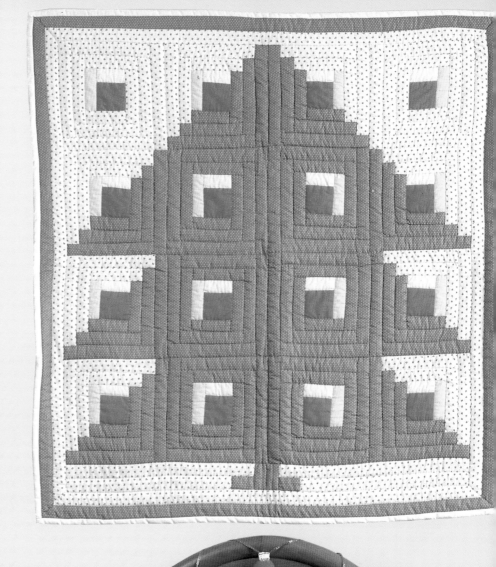

Yuletide Whimsies

*A*s anyone who likes to create a special *Christmas mood in their home can tell you, decorating the Christmas tree often takes up so much time and energy that other areas of the home end up ignored. Sadly, one of the most commonly ignored places is the welcome area, and whether this area in your home is a hallway, a foyer, or a living room, you shouldn't miss out on a great opportunity to set a festive mood for the entire home. Decorating this area needn't be complicated: just arrange a few scrapcraft projects against a backdrop of greenery, ornaments, and a few Christmas cards, and you're done.*

The fabric lights can be arranged around just about any shape — around a doorway or a piece of furniture — and they can be used alone or interwoven with a string of white electric lights. Christmas cards can be attached to the lights' ribbon with clothespins if desired. The miniature stockings are an exciting way to transform small scraps of fabric into something special. Fill them with special tidbits and give them instead of cards, use them as tree ornaments, or place them around the home to add decorative cheer in unusual places. The hand-made, woven-ribbon Christmas card shown here uses a heart pattern to achieve the shape, but simple holiday motifs can also be achieved by using cookie cutters for patterns. While slightly more elaborate than the other projects, the tree skirt and wall hanging are not as time-consuming as you might guess, especially if you opt to do the quilting by machine.

String of Lights

Materials

2 to 4 yards (1.8 to 3.6 m) of narrow ribbon
Scraps of felt in several colors
Stuffing material (batting, scrap stockings, etc.)
Aluminum foil or aluminum pie tins
Craft glue

Instructions

❧ Cut three pieces of the pattern for each bulb and mark the dots as shown with a pencil or pen. With right sides together, sew two pieces together between the dots. Sew the third piece to the first two, stopping at the lower dot.

❧ Turn the right sides out and fill the light with small bits of stuffing. Pack the stuffing tightly in the lower half of the bulb and looser in the upper areas.

❧ Without turning under, pull the upper points firmly together with a needle and thread at points that are level with the upper dots. Tie off when firmly stitched. There should be three points sticking upward. Trim two of the points off about 1/8 of an inch (3 mm) above the stitch point.

❧ Attach the first bulb to the ribbon about 4 inches (10 cm) from the end of the ribbon by folding the remaining point of the bulb over the ribbon and stitching to secure, taking care to make sure the bulb will hang straight. Attach additional bulbs at 8-inch (20 cm) intervals.

❧ Finish the top edges of the bulbs with strips of aluminum foil or the rims of aluminum pie tins that have been cut into 2-1/2- x 2-1/2-inch (6 x 6 cm) strips, and then fold each horizontal edge in to the center to cover any raw edges. Gently slide these pieces above each bulb so that the stitching is covered. Glue the end of each foil piece down and secure the foil to the fabric with a dab of glue if needed. Hang the lights with thumbtacks.

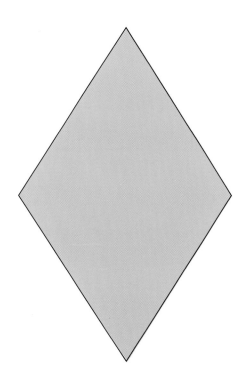

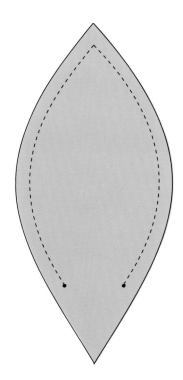

Miniature Stockings

Materials for Each Stocking

*2 scraps of fabric, each measuring approximately
  3 x 4 inches (7 x 10 cm)*
*Scraps of trim, measuring approximately 6 to
  10 inches (15 to 25 cm)*
Scraps of ribbon or cord, measuring 3 to 4 inches
Craft glue

Instructions

With right sides together, cut out the stocking from the pattern and sew. Turn right sides out and gently press. Finish the top of the stocking with a narrow hem. Stitch a loop of ribbon or cord to the back edge of the stocking to form a hanger. Last, glue the trim around the top edge, overlapping at the back. Allow the glue to completely dry before handling the stocking.

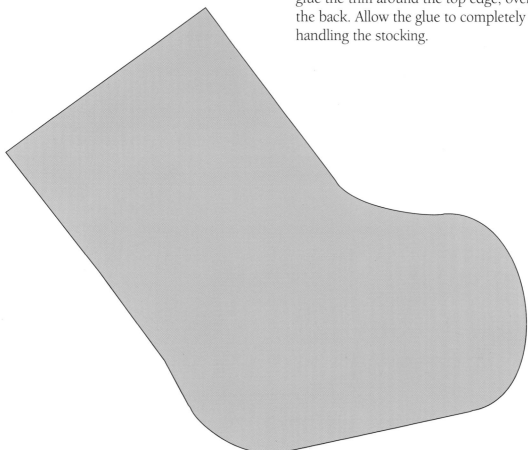

Soft Sculpture Mailbox

Materials

2 pieces of contrasting fabric in 1/2-yard (.5 m)
lengths
Sheet of red or green poster board
Craft glue
Quilt batting
Popsicle stick
Scrap of red fabric for berries

Instructions

🦌 Cut the mailbox body (a rectangle measuring 27 x 12 inches, 68 x 30 cm), end flaps, and holly leaves out of each fabric. Sew one flap section of each fabric together along the curved edge with rights sides facing, leaving the straight edge open. Turn, press, and baste the raw edges together. This will be the door flap.

🦌 For each body piece, sew the narrow ends of the pieces together to form a tube. Press the seam open and turn one piece right side out. Baste the remaining flap pieces together with the wrong sides facing to form the back of the mailbox.

🦌 Pin one body piece to the back piece with the right sides together, matching the seam of the body to the center bottom of the back piece and adjusting the curves to fit. Baste this seam. Fit the remaining body piece to the other right side of the back piece. Pin in place and stitch the seam. When you turn the right sides out, all seam allowances should be hidden and the piece should look reversible.

🦌 Center the door flap over the seam and baste in place with the right sides together. Press the seam allowances on both body pieces under and pin together. Carefully top stitch them together.

🦌 Sew holly leaves (of like fabric) right sides together, leaving an opening for turning. Turn the leaves right sides out, press, and stuff lightly with batting. Blind stitch the edges closed and then machine stitch a curved line down the center. Tack two leaves of the same fabric together at their points and then glue on several red felt berries.

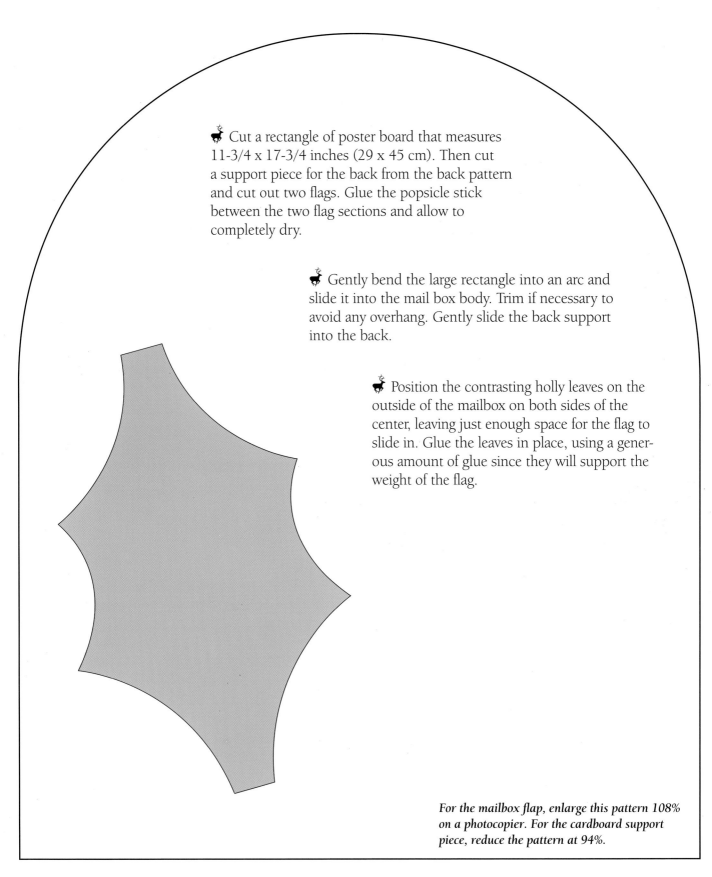

Cut a rectangle of poster board that measures 11-3/4 x 17-3/4 inches (29 x 45 cm). Then cut a support piece for the back from the back pattern and cut out two flags. Glue the popsicle stick between the two flag sections and allow to completely dry.

Gently bend the large rectangle into an arc and slide it into the mail box body. Trim if necessary to avoid any overhang. Gently slide the back support into the back.

Position the contrasting holly leaves on the outside of the mailbox on both sides of the center, leaving just enough space for the flag to slide in. Glue the leaves in place, using a generous amount of glue since they will support the weight of the flag.

For the mailbox flap, enlarge this pattern 108% on a photocopier. For the cardboard support piece, reduce the pattern at 94%.

Tree Skirt

Materials

- 2/3 yard (.6 m) green print fabric
- 2/3 yard red print fabric
- 2/3 yard white with contrasting red, green, and gold print fabric
- 1-1/2 yard (1.4 m) batting or fleece
- 1-1/2 yard lining fabric
- 1/3 yard (.3 m) matching fabric for lining

Instructions

🦌 Cut out the fabric according to the cutting instructions below. Sew one red print and one green print together and press the seam open. Assemble and sew the remaining nine sections in the same way.

To each of the above sections, sew one side at a time of pattern C in place according to the diagram. Sew eight more sections together in the same way. On the last section, leave one side of the triangle unsewn. Sew each of the ten sections together to form the skirt.

Place the lining fabric face up on a flat surface. Place the batting or fleece on top of the lining fabric, and then place the skirt on top of the batting with its right side facing up. Secure the three layers together with pins or basting stitches. Hand or machine quilt the skirt. Trim all sides of the skirt.

Cut four strips measuring 2-1/2 x 44 inches (6 x 110 cm) from the binding fabric. Cut the ends on a 45 degree angle and sew them together. Press in half lengthwise and sew the binding around the skirt, mitering at the corners. Turn the binding to the back and blind stitch in place.

Cutting Instructions

Cut ten pieces from pattern A from the red fabric; ten pieces from pattern B from the green fabric; ten pieces from pattern C from the white fabric. All fabrics must be cut with their right sides facing up.

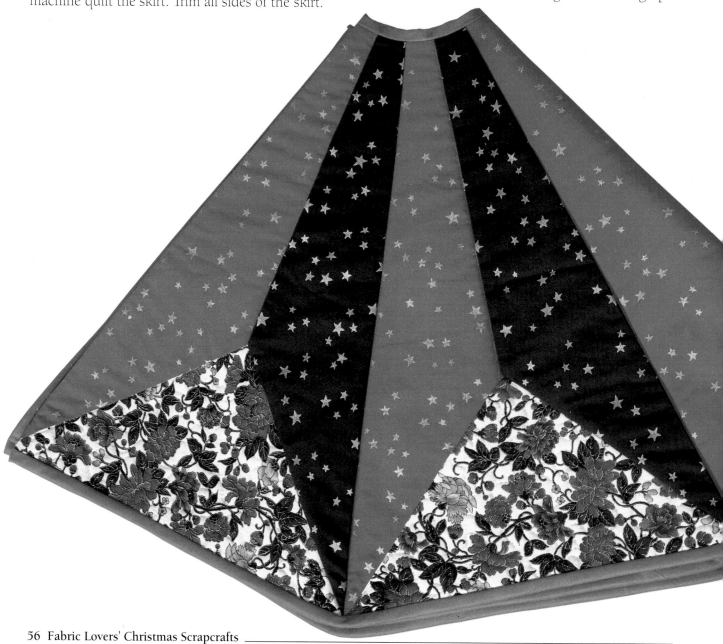

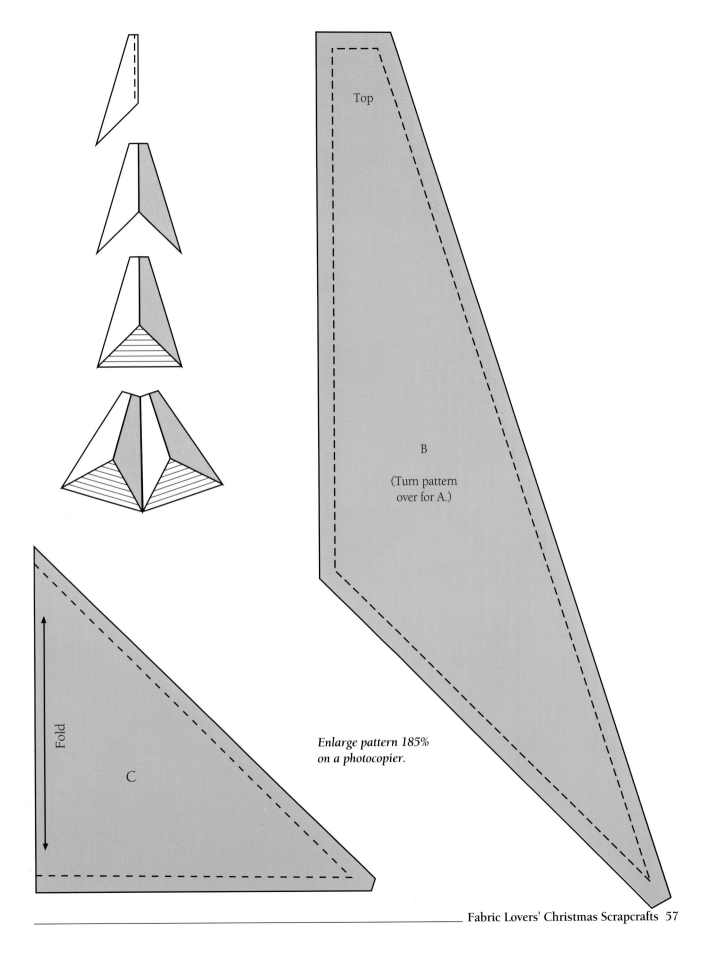

Top

B

(Turn pattern
over for A.)

*Enlarge pattern 185%
on a photocopier.*

Fold

C

Woven Heart Card

Materials

Ribbon scraps in lots of colors
Poster board or cardboard
Craft glue
Paper to frame heart

Instructions

❧ Trace the heart pattern onto the board and cut out. Starting in the center, begin weaving pieces of ribbon in a design you like. Press the ribbon together as you work to ensure a tight weave. Glue down layers of finished areas as you weave to make your work easier and neater. Allow the glue to dry overnight.

❧ Trace the heart shape onto the wrong side of the frame paper. Mark a 1/8-inch (3 mm) border all the way around the heart and then cut out the shape on the inside of this tracing. Carefully glue the woven heart under the edges of the framing paper and allow the glue to completely dry before handling.

Log Cabin Wall Hanging

Materials

6- x 6-inch (15 x 15 cm) square of white fabric

6- x 6-inch square of yellow fabric

12- x 12-inch (30 x 30 cm) square of red fabric

1 yard (.9 m) of white fabric with small red and
green print

1-1/4 yard (1.1 m) green fabric with small white dots

1/3 yard (.3 m) contrasting fabric for binding

1-1/4 yards batting or fleece

1-1/4 yards lining fabric

Instructions

🦌 Cut out the fabric according to the cutting instructions on page 63. Begin each of the 16 blocks with a red square. Sew the yellow strip to the red square on the side designated in the diagrams. Next, sew the white strip, and then follow with the green or white print cut to length. Following the diagrams, continue sewing strips and cutting them to the correct length until the block is finished. When finished, you should have three blocks pieced like diagram A, one block pieced like diagram B, four blocks pieced like diagram C, one block pieced like diagram D, four blocks pieced like diagram E, and three blocks pieced like diagram F.

🦌 Arrange and sew the blocks so they form the pattern shown in the photo. Press well. Sew one of the white strips to each side and the top of the square. To form the base of the tree on the bottom side, cut two of the white strips in half and sew a 2-1/2-inch length of the green print between them, and then sew a 4-1/2-inch (11 cm) length of the green print between the next two sections. Center the strip with the 2-1/2-inch green section to the bottom of the square and sew. Center the next strip with the larger green section under the previous strip and sew. Now sew a plain section of the white under the last strip. Border each side of the piece with one of the 2- x 44-inch strips and miter the corners.

🦌 Place the lining on a flat surface with its right side facing down. Place the batting or fleece on top of the backing, and then place the pieced squares on top of the batting with its right side facing up. Secure the three layers together with pins or basting stitches. Hand or machine quilt in the ditch of the pieces. Trim the lining and batting to match the top.

🦌 Sew the four 2-1/2- x 44-inch binding strips together on a 45 degree angle. Press the binding in half lengthwise and sew it to the right side of the quilt, mitering the corners. Turn to the backside and blind stitch in place.

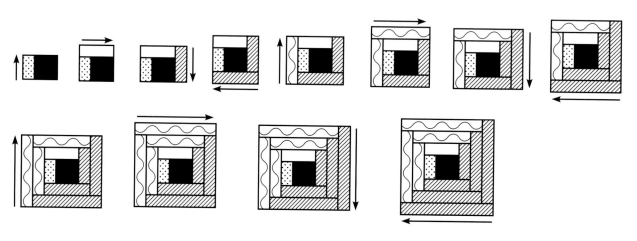

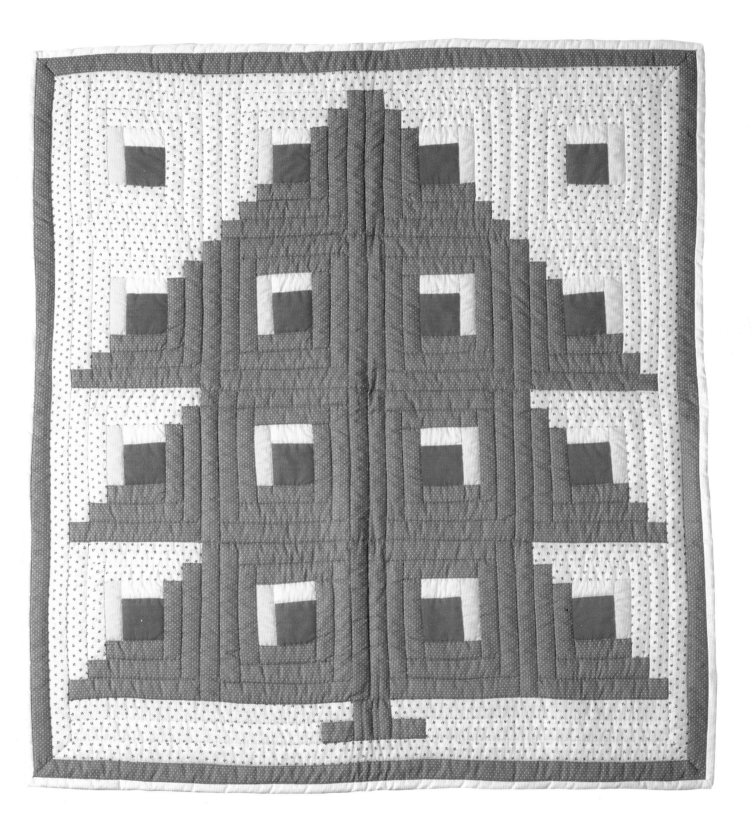

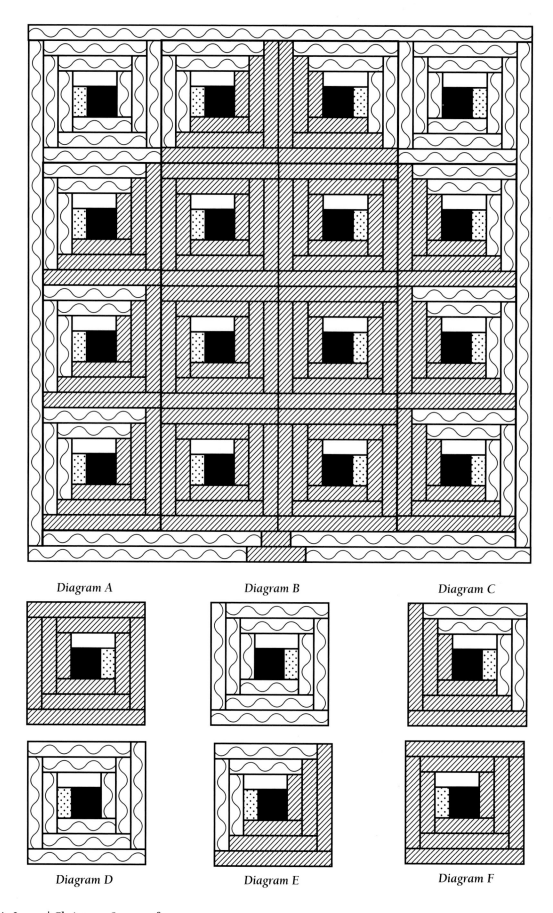

Diagram A   Diagram B   Diagram C

Diagram D   Diagram E   Diagram F

Cutting Instructions

🦌 Cut 16 rectangles measuring 1-1/2 x 3-1/2 inches (4 x 8 cm) from the white fabric. Cut 16 rectangles measuring 1-1/2 x 2-1/2 inches (4 x 6 cm) from the yellow fabric. Cut 16 squares measuring 2-1/2 x 2-1/2 inches (6 x 6 cm) from the red fabric. Cut 22 strips measuring 1-1/2 x 44 inches (4 x 110 cm) from the white print fabric. Cut 24 strips measuring 1-1/2 x 44 inches from the green print fabric; cut 4 strips measuring 2 x 44 inches (5 x 110 cm) from the green print fabric. Cut 4 strips measuring 2-1/2 x 44 inches (6 x 110 cm) from the binding fabric.

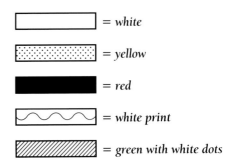

☐	= white
⣿	= yellow
■	= red
〜	= white print
⫽	= green with white dots

Culinary Celebrations

*B*etween guests and special baking projects, most of us spend far more time in the kitchen around the holidays than we might like, so decorating this room can revitalize your spirits and give you a much-needed boost of creative energy. And while several of the projects shown here require considerable sewing time, keep in mind that decorating the kitchen in following years will be as simple as unpacking a box.

The basket liner transforms an inexpensive mushroom basket into a useful container for fruits, nuts, and other holiday tidbits. The basket can be used year 'round if you line the holiday fabric with a fabric that complements your kitchen's decor. The potholder is another quick project, and you might want to consider making several to give as hostess gifts when you're out visiting. The apron and tablecloth require larger time investments, but they'll make wonderful keepsakes for generations to come.

Potholder

Materials

1/4 yard (.2 m) each of two contrasting fabrics
1/3 yard (.3 m) of contrasting striped fabric
2 12- x 12-inch (30 x 30 cm) squares of quilt batting
Contrasting binding
Plastic ring or magnet

Instructions

🦌 Cut out the fabric according to the cutting instructions below. Sew the triangles together according to the piecing diagram shown with the apron and press the seams open. Sew the squares and pieced triangles together in strips as shown and press the seams open. Sew the strips together to form a square. Sew the strips to the four sides of each square, mitering the corners. Press well.

🦌 Place the plain fabric square right side down on a flat surface and place two squares of batting on top of it. Place the patchwork square on top of the batting, right side up. Quilt the three layers together by hand or machine and trim the batting. Sew a binding around the edges of the potholder. Attach a 1-inch (2-1/2 cm) plastic ring to one corner for hanging or glue a magnet to the back of one corner.

Cutting Instructions

🦌 From one of the 1/4-yard fabric pieces, cut a square measuring 12 x 12 inches, two squares from pattern A, and eight triangles from pattern B. From the other 1/4-yard fabric piece, cut eight squares from pattern A and eight triangles from pattern B. From the 1/3-yard fabric piece, cut eight strips measuring 1-1/2 x 12 inches (4 x 30 cm).

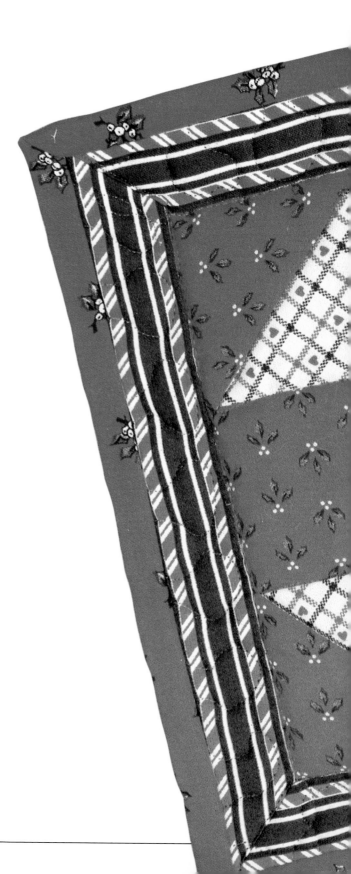

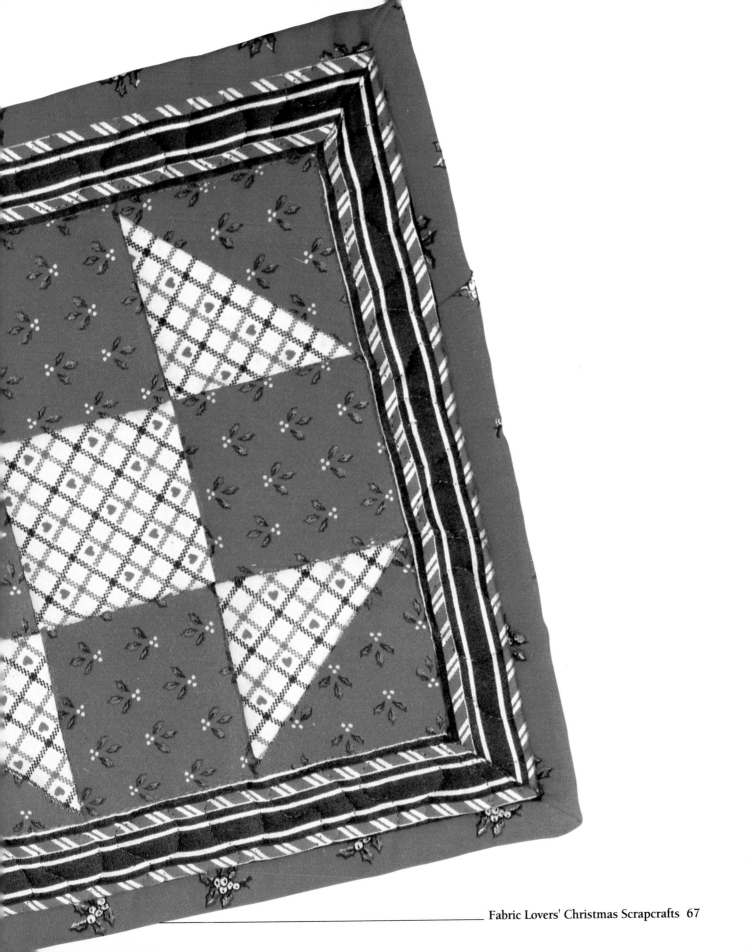

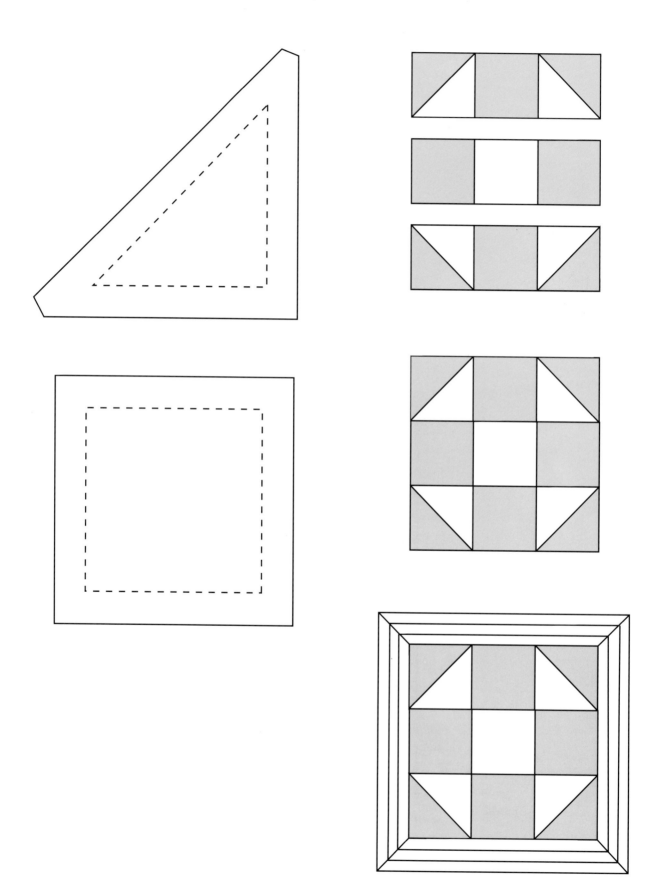

Gift Basket Liners

Materials

Oblong mushroom basket
3/8 yard (.3 m) holiday print fabric
1-1/8 yard (1 m) gathered lace or ruffled trim

Instructions

🦌 Cut two rectangles from the fabric measuring 10-1/2 x 19-1/2 inches (26 x 49 cm). Place right sides together and sew a half-inch (1-1/4 cm) seam along one of the long sides. Press the seam open. Sew both of the shorter sides together and press the seams open.

🦌 Sew the trim to the long open edge, overlapping and trimming where the ends meet. Press the seam down and top-stitch on the right side of the fabric 1/4-inch (2/3 cm) from the pressed edge of the fabric. Place the liner in the basket and fill with holiday goodies or decorations.

Apron

Materials

    1 yard (.9 m) of fabric for skirt
    1/4 yard (.2 m) of contrasting fabric
    1/3 yard (.3 m) of contrasting striped or other fabric
    2 12-x 12-inch (30 x 30 cm) squares of quilt batting
    Sewing and quilting thread

Instructions

🦌 Cut out the fabric according to the cutting instructions on page 71. Sew the triangles together according to the piecing diagram and press the seams open. Sew the squares and pieced triangles together in strips as shown and press the seams open. Sew the strips together to form a square. Repeat to form a second square. Take the 3- x 12-inch strips and sew them to the four sides of each square, mitering the corners. Press well.

🦌 Place the 12- x 12-inch square of batting on the table and place the 12- x 12-inch square of the main fabric right side up on top of the batting. Then place the pieced square right side down on top of the fabric square. Secure the three layers together with pins and stitch them together on three sides, leaving the fourth side open. Trim the batting, turn the right sides out, and press.

🦌 Repeat the above step with the second patchwork square and the plain fabric, but this time making a 4-inch (10 cm) slit in the square of plain fabric. Place the three layers for the square as directed above and then sew all four sides. Trim the batting close to the seam and turn the right sides out through the 4-inch slit. This square will be used for the pocket of the apron. Quilt the two squares by hand or machine.

🦌 Take the two 2-1/2- x 22-inch strips and fold each one in half to measure 1-1/4 x 22 inches (3 x 55 cm). Sew each strip on the raw edge side and across one end. Turn and press. These will be attached to the bib square as shown. Place the two 2-1/2- x 16-1/2 strips along the bottom of the bib

as shown, one on each side. You may want to sew a strip of interfacing or batting along with the strips to strengthen the waistband. Press well.

🦌 Hem each of the 5- x 44-inch strips along their long sides and across one end to form the apron's ties. Pleat the raw end of the ties and sew into each end of the waistband.

🦌 Hem each long side of the large fabric rectangle and then turn up a 4-inch hem on one of the shorter sides. Position the quilted pocket on one side of the skirt about 8 inches (20 cm) from the side and 6 inches (15 cm) from the top. Sew in place.

🦌 Gather the top of the skirt until it fits the waistband and sew it to the front section of the waistband. Turn to the back and turn under a 1/4-inch (6 mm) seam of the back side of the band. Hand stitch in place.

Cutting Instructions

🦌 From the 1-yard fabric piece, cut a rectangle measuring 29 x 44 inches (72 x 110 cm), two strips measuring 5 x 44 inches (12 x 110 cm), two strips measuring 2-1/2 x 22 inches (6 x 55 cm), two strips measuring 2-1/2 x 16-1/2 inches (6 x 42 cm), two squares measuring 12 x 12 inches (30 x 30 cm), two squares from pattern A, and eight triangles from pattern B. From the 1/4-yard fabric piece, cut eight squares from pattern A and eight triangles from pattern B. From the 1/3-yard fabric piece, cut eight strips measuring 3 x 12 inches (7 x 30 cm).

Note: A patchwork pillow can be made to match the apron and potholder by first piecing four blocks together with inch-wide (2-1/2 cm) strips of a contrasting fabric. Next, border the outside of the large block with 1-1/2-inch-wide (4 cm) strips. Quilt the pillow top as you did the apron pocket. Cut a piece of contrasting fabric to the same size as the pillow top and stitch it to the pillow top with right sides together, leaving a small opening for turning. Turn the pillow right sides out, stuff, and slip stitch the opening closed.

Tablecloth

Materials

- 2-1/2 yards (2.3 m) green with smaller print
- 2-1/2 yards red with small dots fabric
- 1/3 yard (.3 m) green with larger print
- 1/4 yard (.2 m) white with small red and green print fabric
- 1-3/4 yards (1.6 m) white fabric
- 4 yards (3.6 m) backing fabric
- 4 yards of batting
- 2/3 yard (.6 m) of coordinating fabric for binding

Instructions

🦌 Mark off a piece of paper measuring 34 x 44 inches (86 x 110 cm) into 2-inch (5 cm) squares. Using the illustration on page 75 for a guide, use a straight edge and a pencil to construct one-fourth of the tablecloth's design. Trace your pattern piece outlines onto a second piece of paper and add a 1/4-inch (6 mm) seam allowance on all sides.

🦌 Cut out the fabric according to the cutting instructions on page 74. Begin piecing by sewing the four D patterns together as shown in diagram 1. Sew pattern pieces E to each side of the previous section as shown in diagram 2. Join pattern pieces A to the top and bottom of diagram 2's block. Now join pieces B to each side of diagram 2's block.

🦌 Sew pattern pieces F, C, and G together twice, as shown in diagram 4. Reverse the order and sew the other two sections together. Sew the sections of diagram 4 to the designated places in diagram 3 as shown in diagram 5.

🦌 Sew the 2-1/2- x 45-inch strips to each of the narrow sides of diagram 5. Sew the 2-1/2- x 62-inch strips to each of the longer sides. Miter the corners and trim. Sew the 6-1/2- x 54-inch strips to the narrow sides. Sew the 6-1/2- x 74-inch strips to the longer sides. Miter the corners and trim.

🦌 Sew the red and green fabrics of pattern H (the border triangles) in alternating order. Look at the full-size diagram on page 75 to see how many you'll need for each side. Sew the squares when you're sewing the ends together on the 1/2 of H sides. Continue sewing to the end of the section to complete the top of the tablecloth.

🦌 Cut the backing fabric into two 2-yard pieces. Sew the pieces together on the selvage sides before sewing. Press, and cut off the selvage edges. Place the backing fabric right side down on a large, flat surface. Place the batting on top of the backing fabric, and then place the patchworked piece on top of the batting with its right side facing up. Secure the three layers together with pins or large basting stitches. Hand or machine quilt.

🦌 After quilting, trim all sides to match the top. Then sew the eight strips of binding together and press their seams. Fold the seam down at each end, and then press the entire strip wrong sides together in half on all eight strips. Sew the strips to the top of the table-cloth as shown, mitering the corners on the binding. Turn the binding to the back side over the raw edges and blind stitch to the back of the tablecloth.

Cutting Instructions

🦌 From the small-print green fabric: cut four of pattern C; cut two strips measuring 2-1/2 x 62 inches (6 x 155 cm); cut two strips measuring 2-1/2 x 42 inches (6 x 105 cm); cut 64 of pattern H. From the red with small dots fabric: cut two of pattern A; cut two of pattern B; cut 64 of pattern H; cut two strips measuring 6-1/2 x 74 inches (16 x 185 cm); cut two strips measuring 6-1/2 x 54 inches (16 x 135 cm).

🦌 From the larger-print green fabric: cut four of pattern D; cut four squares measuring 6-1/2 x 6-1/2 inches (16 x 16 cm). From the red-and-green-print white fabric: cut four of pattern E.

🦌 From the white fabric: cut four of pattern F; cut four of pattern G. For the binding: cut eight strips measuring 2-1/2 x 45 inches (6 x 112 cm) on the crosswise grain. Cut the ends on a 45 degree angle.

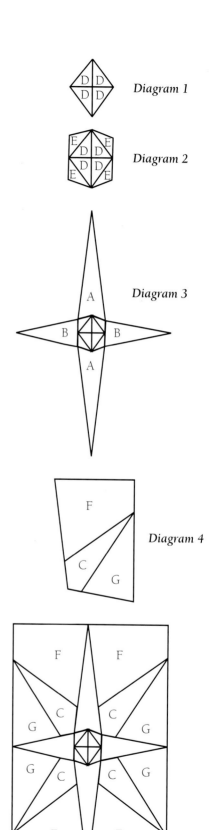

Diagram 1

Diagram 2

Diagram 3

Diagram 4

Diagram 5

Green with small print	*Red with small dots*	*Green with large print*	*White with red and green print*	*White*

Santa's Treasures

*C*elebrating the magic of Santa
Claus has been a part of
American Christmas celebrations since
the colonial days, and the tradition
dates back much earlier in European
countries. Santa's presence alone has
been known to build anticipation and
excitement in children who believe
they've been good all year. As a symbol
of giving and festivity, Santa makes
the perfect decorating icon, and even
the family pets can get caught up
in the excitement.

  The Santa projects in this chapter
feature versatility. The rug can double
as a wall hanging or a table decoration. The Santa napkin rings can be
placed over a drinking glass and
arranged around the home in all
sorts of out-of-the-way places, while
the spool Santa makes a fun knickknack or tree ornament. The chapter
also includes several projects that
make quick, fun gifts.

Santa Rug

Materials

   2 yards (1.8 m) red fur
   1 yard (.9 m) white fur
   Fabric glue (optional)
   Glue gun
   1/4 yard (.2 m) green felt
   Stuffing material
   4 large black buttons
   Black belt*
   Fabric Paints
   Cotton balls
   1 yard of cream muslin
   Cotton batting
   Paint pens
   Cosmetic powder blush

Instructions for Santa's Body

🦌 Cut off a 3-inch (7-1/2 cm) strip from the bottom of the red fur and set it aside. From the white fur, cut two 4-inch-wide (10 cm) strips that are the same length as the large piece of red fur. Position the white strips in the top middle of the red fur and pin them down until you're about three-fourths of the way down. Then curve the fur outward and pin in place. Secure the strips in place with fabric glue or large basting stitches.

🦌 Use an adult's hand as a pattern to cut out the mittens from the green felt. Cut out two pieces for each hand, place them right sides together, and sew. Clip the seams and turn the mittens right sides out. Position the belt across the red fur and secure in place with hot glue. (*Note: The belt can be purchased or it can be made from black felt.) Cut two strips measuring 1 x 3 inches (2-1/2 x 7-1/2 cm) from the piece of leftover red fur. Position the strips over the belt and secure them with fabric glue or hand stitching.

🦌 Stuff both mittens until they're slightly full. Position them under the belt at an angle on either side of the rug, and glue or tack in place. Cut two 3- x 6-inch (7 x 15 cm) strips from the white fur. Position the strips over the mittens, and secure in place with fabric glue or basting stitches. Arrange and attach the buttons down the front of Santa's jacket. Next, create a slightly tapered waistline by running a row of gathering stitches under the belt. Pull the thread until you're happy with the shape, and then tie off the threads.

Instructions for Santa's Head

🦌 With right sides together, sew three sides of two 24- x 24-inch (60 cm) muslin squares together. Turn right sides out and stuff with cotton batting. Create a three-dimensional nose by picking up a few of the muslin threads with a needle and thread from the wrong side of the muslin and pushing the threads into the batting. Next, add the eyes and mouth with paint pens, and add blush to the cheeks.

🦌 Using a sandwich plate as a pattern, cut out a circle from the muslin. Measure the distance around the circle, add 1/2 inch (13 mm), and cut out a strip that's this length and 2 inches (5 cm) wide. Form Santa's neck by placing the strip upright and hot-gluing it to the edges of the circle. Gather the bottom of Santa's head and arrange it inside the neck, and then secure it in place with glue and stitches.

🦌 To make Santa's beard, gently pull the cotton batting to form a shape you like, and then glue it to a backing of muslin. Hot-glue the muslin under Santa's nose. Last, pin a hat to the top of his head. (You can use a ready-made hat or make one by sewing two triangles together and trimming the edges and top with cotton batting.)

Spool Santa

Materials

Large thread spool, plastic or wood
Scraps of yarn in pink, red, and black
Craft glue
Scraps of construction paper in black and red
Cotton ball

Instructions

🦌 Coat the top third of the spool with a layer of craft glue and then tightly wrap the pink yarn around the spool. Cover the remaining portion of the spool with glue and then tightly wrap the yarn down the spool. Next, loop the black yarn around the middle of the spool and glue it in place to form Santa's belt.

🦌 Cut out two small circles from the black construction paper to form the eyes and another circle in the same size from the red paper to form the nose. Position and glue them in place. Cut out a semi-circle from the red construction paper and fold it into a cone to form a hat shape to fit the inside edge of the spool's top. Glue the hat in place and allow to dry. Divide the cotton ball into three separate pieces for the pom-pom, hat trim, and beard, and then glue them in place.

Santa Napkin Rings

Materials for Each Santa

*Red dinner napkin or scrap of red fabric cut
to a 18- x 18-inch (46 x 46 cm) square*
Scrap of white felt
Scrap of pink felt
Plastic craft eyes or two black beads
Red bead
Craft glue or Velcro tabs

Instructions

🦌 Cut out the Santa shape from the white felt and
then cut out a 1-1/2- x 1-inch (4 x 2-1/2 cm) rectangle from the pink felt. Position the right side of the
pink felt against the wrong side of the white felt so
that it covers the face opening and glue in place. Position the eyes and nose in place and secure with glue.

🦌 With the right side facing up, fold the napkin or
fabric square in half to form a rectangle and press
well. Fold it again to form a square and press well.
Tilt the square so it forms a diamond and then fold
the left and right corners in toward the center. The
corners will overlap about 2 inches (5 cm) on the
back side. Turn the napkin over, position the Santa
in place, and then wrap the bands around each
side to meet in the back. Secure the bands with
glue to make a standing Santa, or with Velcro to
make a napkin ring.

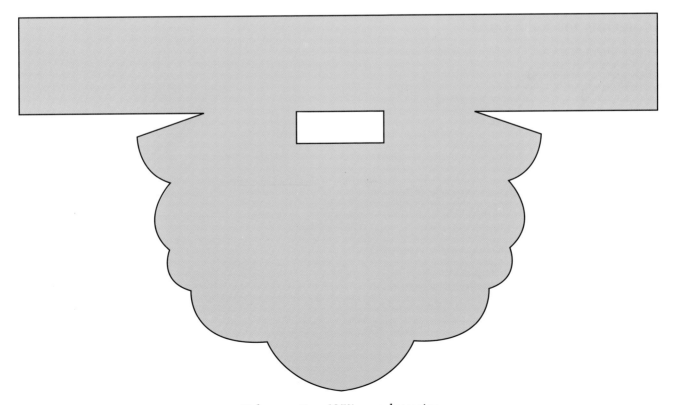

Enlarge pattern 125% on a photocpier.

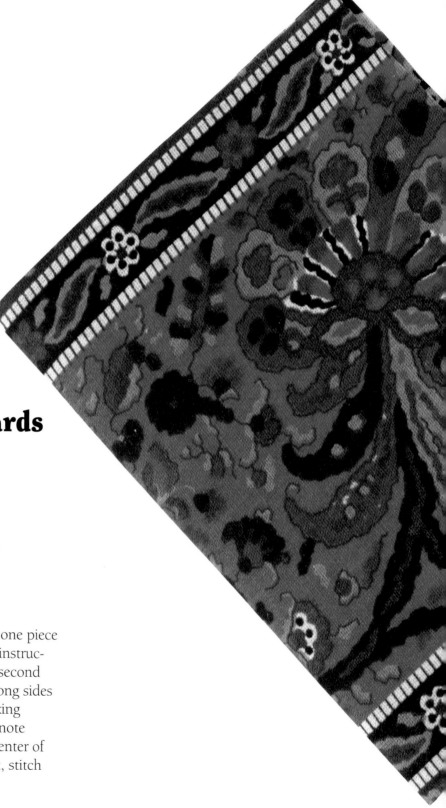

Fabric Greeting Cards

Materials for Each Card

*2 scraps of fabric cut to 7-1/2 x 5 inches
(18 x 12 cm)
Iron-on webbing
Sheet of note paper cut to 7 x 4-1/2 inches
(17 x 11 cm)*

Instructions

🦌 Iron the webbing to the wrong side of one piece of fabric according to the manufacturer's instructions and remove after cooling. Place the second piece of fabric on top of the first, with wrong sides facing, and iron. Trim the fabric with pinking shears, fold it in half, and press. Fold the note paper in half and then position it in the center of the fabric card so the fold lines align. Last, stitch the paper in place down the fold line.

Fabric Tree

Materials

*1/3 yard (.3 m) holiday print fabric (prints
    may be mixed, if desired)*
*Foam cone (The cone used in this project is
    6-1/2 inches, 16 cm, tall, but any size
    cone will work as long as you make
    appropriate changes in fabric quantities.)*
Metal-tip sewing pins
Gold thread

Instructions

🦌 Begin by wrapping an inch-wide (2-1/2 cm)
strip of fabric around the bottom of the tree, allow-
ing about a 1/4 inch (6 mm) of fabric overhang on
the bottom side. Secure the top edge of the fabric
in place with pins and then secure the bottom edge
of the fabric by folding it underneath the cone and
pinning in place. Cut out a triangle that's 3 inches
(7 cm) wide at its base. Fold it in half, right sides
together, and stitch. Turn the right sides out and
fold under a 1/4-inch hem at the bottom. This
piece will be used later to cover the top of the tree.

🦌 Cut the remaining fabric into 1-3/4- x 1-3/4
inch (45 mm) squares. Fold each square as shown
in the illustrations. Begin pinning the folded
squares to the tree with their points facing down.
Start at the bottom and work your way up, and be
sure to position the points of the squares in each
adjacent row so that they fill the gaps formed in the
previous row. Stop attaching the squares when
there's approximately 1 inch of foam at the top. Fit
the fabric top over the tip of the tree and tie in
place with several thicknesses of gold thread.

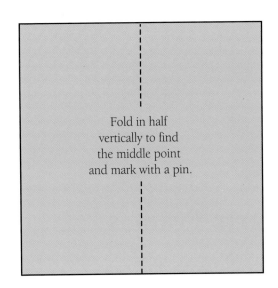

Fold in half
vertically to find
the middle point
and mark with a pin.

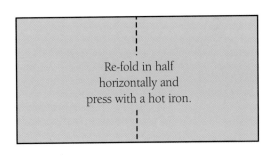

Re-fold in half
horizontally and
press with a hot iron.

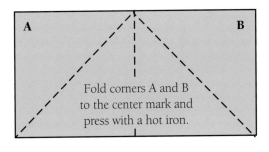

A   B

Fold corners A and B
to the center mark and
press with a hot iron.

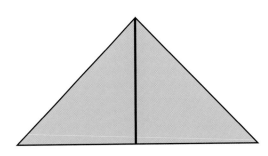

Fabric Frames

Materials for Each Frame

Double-mat picture set
1/4 yard (.2 m) fabric
Batting
Craft glue

Instructions

🦌 Place the top mat face down on the wrong side of your fabric. Turn the fabric over to make sure the pattern is square with the frame. Turn the fabric back over and trace the shape of the mat with a felt tip pen. Mark off an additional 5/8 inch (15 mm) on all sides for a wrap allowance. Draw a diagonal line with a straight edge through the opening in the mat from each top corner to each bottom corner to form an X.

🦌 Remove the mat and cut out the fabric, making sure not to cut too deeply into the diagonal X lines. Replace the mat over the fabric and draw a second line that's 5/8 of an inch in from the inside edge of the mat. Cut off the excess fabric along these lines.

🦌 Trace the inner and outer edges of the top mat onto a double thickness of batting and cut it out. Glue the batting to the front of this mat, and place the fabric over the batting. Fold the fabric over the edges and glue them to the back of the mat. Glue the bottom mat to the back of the top mat, taking care to leave about half an inch (13 mm) of the inner edges unglued so the picture will slide in.

"Meow" and "Woof" Stockings

Materials

1 yard (.9 m) white pre-quilted fabric
Quilt batting
Scraps of red and green cotton fabric
Acrylic fabric paints
Puff paints
Threads
Iron-on webbing
Polyform clay
White paint
Gold cording

Instructions

🦌 Cut out four stocking shapes from the quilted fabric (two for each stocking). Cut out a strip of red and green fabric and sew them together lengthwise. Next, cut a piece of batting to fit the red and green piece and stitch the batting to the wrong side. Sew the red edge to the top of the front side of the stocking and press.

🦌 Cut out the cat, dog, mouse, and ball shapes. Attach the iron-on webbing to their wrong sides and paint them. After the paint has completely dried, iron the shapes onto the stocking fronts and satin stitch around the edges.

🦌 Stitch the front and back stocking pieces together with right sides facing. Turn right sides out and press. Hand sew a 1-1/2-inch (4 cm) hem around the top. Make paw prints across the top of the stockings with black paint.

🦌 Shape the clay into two bones. Make a hole with a toothpick in the top right corner and bake as directed. Paint the bones white. After they dry, use puff paints to write "Meow" and "Woof" on them. Last, thread a piece of gold cording through the holes and attach them to the stockings.

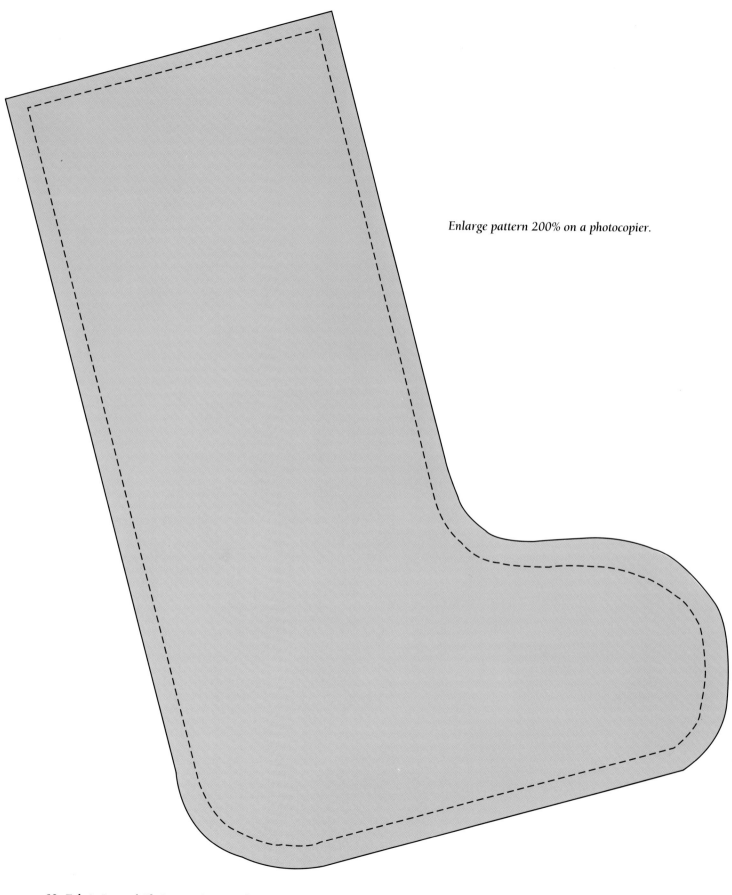

Enlarge pattern 200% on a photocopier.

Album Slip Cover

Materials

*1/8 to 1/2 yard (.1 to .5 m) of fabric,
    depending on the size of your album*
Old Christmas cards
Craft glue

Instructions

🦌 Measure the height and width of your album. Add 1/2 inch (13 mm) to the height measurement and 4-1/2 inches (11 cm) to the width measurement, and cut out the fabric. Fold down and sew a 1/4-inch (6 mm) hem on both sides of the fabric. With the right side facing up, fold over each side of the fabric 2 inches (5 cm) to form the flaps. Pin the ends and stitch with a 1/4-inch seam. Turn the flaps right side out and press well. Hem the top and bottom edges as you did the sides. Last, decorate the front of the slip cover with colorful motifs cut out from Christmas cards and glue them in place.

Irresistible Patchwork

*F*or many people, unpacking the
Christmas tablecloth and arranging
it on the dining room table represents
the beginning of the holiday season.
For fabric scrapcrafters, though, this
is just too easy. Decorating the dining
room table offers a myriad of irresistible
craft opportunities that can create an
enchanting table setting for both guests
and family members to enjoy.

The dining room table shown here
is decorated with quilted place mats
made from a mountain star pattern.
Extra blocks of the same pattern were
assembled to form a table runner and
window valances. The quilt blocks can
be lined with a fabric that complements your dining room's non-holiday
decor so they can be used year 'round.
The casserole carriers are made from
kitchen towels and take just a few minutes to assemble. For crafters with lots
of small scraps, the barrette and magnet projects will be great fun.

Mountain Star Place Mats, Table Runner, and Valances

Materials for All Three Projects

1 yard (.9 m) red print fabric
1 yard green print fabric
*2 yards (1.8 m) white-with-small-red-and-green-dots
    fabric*
2 yards of a second red print fabric
3-1/3 yards (3 m) lining fabric
3 yards (2.7 m) batting or fleece

Instructions

🦌 Cut out the fabric according to the cutting instructions on page 98. Be sure to note that the first two fabrics need to be cut from single layers of fabric for the geometric patterns to correctly fit together.

🦌 To make a square, sew B and C together on the notched side, stopping 1/4 inch (6 mm) from the edge as shown in diagram 1 on page 101. Repeat this step four times and press. Next, sew pattern D to each of the four sections and press.

🦌 Pin piece A to the pieces you just assembled as shown in iagram 3 on page 101. Sew from the tip of B to the point where you left B and C open. Flip A to the other side and sew from the tip of C to the point and press. Repeat this process on the other three sections.

🦌 To assemble the final block, sew the four sections together to form a rectangle. You will need four rectangle blocks for the place mats, two rectangle blocks for the table runner, and three rectangle blocks for each valance.

🦌 *To finish the place mats,* sew the 1-1/2-inch strips of border print to each of the rectangle's four sides, mitering the corners as you work. Place the rectangle of lining right side facing down on a flat surface. Then place the batting on top of the lining, and place the pieced rectangle right side up on top of the batting. Pin or baste the layers together.

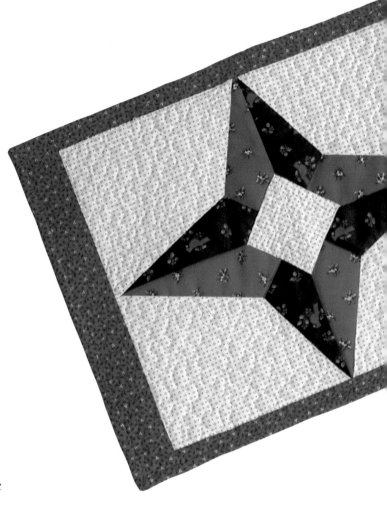

🦌 Machine or hand quilt each place mat. Trim the edges of the place mat. Cut the ends of the 2-1/2 inch strips at a 45 degree angle. Sew them to make one continuous strip. Then fold the strip in half and press. Sew the binding to the right side of the placemat. Miter the corners and turn the binding back and blind stitch in place.

🦌 *To finish the table runner,* sew a 1-1/2-inch strip to the 12-inch (30 cm) side of a rectangle block.

Flip the strip and sew another rectangle to the strip. Border your two-rectangle piece with a 1-1/2-inch strip, mitering the corners as you work. Place the lining fabric right side facing down on a flat surface. Place the batting or fleece on top of the lining fabric, and then place the table runner right side up on top of the batting. Pin or baste the layers together. Machine or hand quilt and bind the edges as you did with the place mats.

🦌 *To finish the valances,* assemble the rectangles and add borders as shown in the illustration on page 100. Your finished valance should be 9 inches (22 cm) longer than your rod for a good fit, so you may need to make some adjustments in the width of the borders for a custom fit. Finish the valance as you did the place mats and table runner. Make the curtain casing by pressing all four sides down 1/2 inch (13 mm) and then sewing it across the top of the valance on the back side.

Cutting Instructions

🦌 Cut out 24 of pattern B from the first red print fabric; the pattern needs to be placed right side up on the right side of the fabric; cutting the pieces from folded fabric will not work. Also cut out 24 pieces of pattern C; the pattern needs to be placed wrong side up on a single layer of fabric.

🦌 Cut out 24 of pattern B from a single layer of the green print fabric with the pattern wrong side up; cutting the pieces from folded fabric will not work. Cut out 24 of pattern C from a single layer of the green fabric with the right side up.

🦌 From the white-with-green-and-red-dot fabric, cut 48 from pattern D and 48 from pattern A. From the second red print fabric, cut six strips across the fabric that are 3-1/2 inches (9 cm) wide (for the valances); cut ten strips across the fabric that are 1-1/2 inches (4 cm) wide for the place mats and table runner; cut two strips across the fabric that are 6 inches (15 cm) wide for the outside borders of the valances; cut 13 strips across the fabric that are 2-1/2 inches (6 cm) wide for the binding; cut four strips measuring 6-1/2 x 22 inches (16 x 25 cm) for the curtain's tiebacks.

🦌 From the lining fabric, cut two rectangles measuring 22 x 54 inches (55 x 136 cm) for the valances; cut one rectangle measuring 16 x 29 inches (41 x 72 cm) for the table runner; cut four rectangles measuring 16 x 18 inches (41 x 46 cm) for the place mats; and cut two strips measuring 4 x 54 inches (10 x 136 cm) for the curtain rod casing. From the batting or fleece, cut the same rectangles as you did for the lining fabric, except for the curtain rod casing.

Valance Assembly Diagram

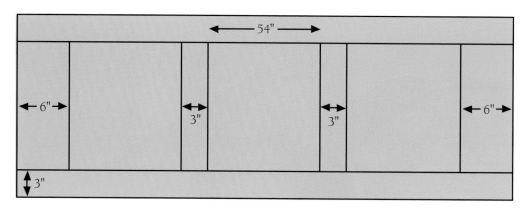

Tip: Cut two rectangles large enough to fit inside a box from leftover scraps of fabric. With right sides together, sew the rectangles together on all sides, leaving a hole large enough for turning open. Turn the rectangle right sides out, press, and glue or slip stitch the opening closed. Crafters who like to paint may enjoy echoing a motif from the fabric on the top and sides of the box.

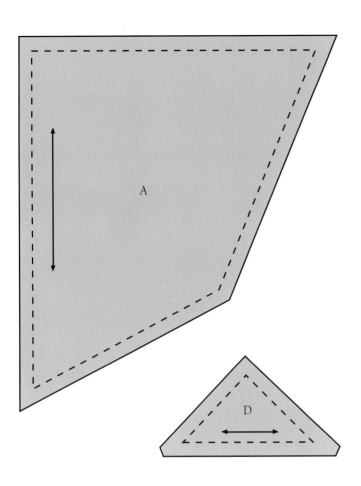

A

D

Enlarge all patterns 200% on a photocopier.

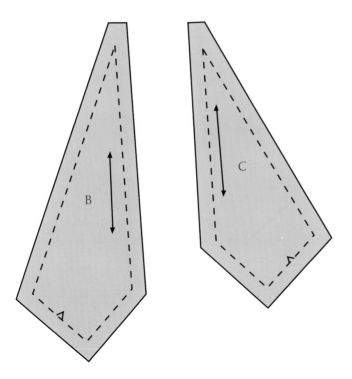

B

C

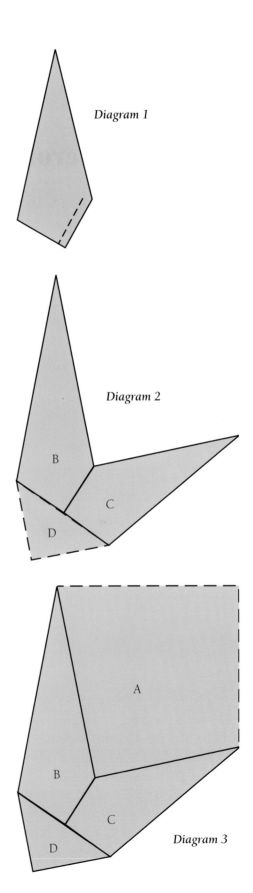

Diagram 1

Diagram 2

B

C

D

A

B

C

D

Diagram 3

Pocket Casserole Carrier

Materials

2 terry cloth dish towels in a holiday print

Instructions

🦌 Place the two towels end to end, overlapping them so that the total remaining length is about 37 inches (93 cm). The overlap area will be your seam allowance. Sew in the overlapped position or adjust the towels so that they'll be sewn right sides together.

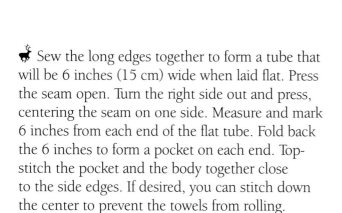

🦌 Sew the long edges together to form a tube that will be 6 inches (15 cm) wide when laid flat. Press the seam open. Turn the right side out and press, centering the seam on one side. Measure and mark 6 inches from each end of the flat tube. Fold back the 6 inches to form a pocket on each end. Top-stitch the pocket and the body together close to the side edges. If desired, you can stitch down the center to prevent the towels from rolling.

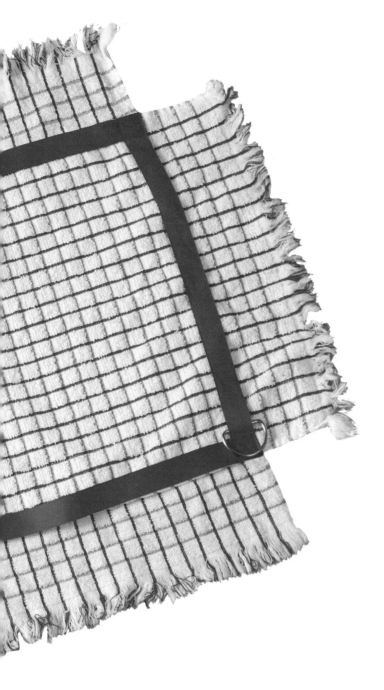

Casserole Carrier

Materials

2 terry cloth dish or hand towels
2-1/8 yards (1.9 m) of 1-inch (2-1/2 cm)
  grosgrain ribbon
2 craft rings, 2 inches (5 cm) in diameter

Instructions

🦌 Working on a flat surface, arrange the two towels on top of each other at right angles so that a square is formed in the center and the overlapping ends are equal. Pin the towels together and top stitch around the outside edge of the square. Make a second row of top stitching 1/4-inch (6 mm) inside the first row.

🦌 Starting in one corner, place the ribbon along the top stitching, pinning as you go and folding the ribbon at the corners so it lays flat. When you reach the starting point, fold and tuck the ribbon to imitate the other corners.

🦌 Place a pin in each of the corner folds. Pin down two opposite corners. For each of the two remaining corners, lift and insert the craft ring through the ribbon, and then pin the corners in the same position as the first two. Your rings should be on diagonally opposite corners.

🦌 Top stitch each corner spot around the edges of the square, and then sew an X within each little square. To use the holder, place the casserole dish in the middle of the towels, draw the two rings up over the dish, and grasp the ribbons at the top. The ends of the towels will fall like a skirt around the edges of the dish.

Braided Holiday Barrette

Materials

3-1/2-inch (8 cm) barrette base
3 fabric scraps cut to 3 x 8 inches (7 x 20 cm)
Ribbon or other narrow trim
Old stockings, toe and hip portions cut off
Safety pin

Instructions

🦌 Fold each piece of fabric in half lengthwise and stitch along the long end to form a tube. Attach a safety pin to one end of the stocking leg and use it to pull the stocking through the fabric tube. Do not stretch the stocking unless you want a bunched-up effect.

🦌 Trim the protruding length of stocking about 1/2 inch (13 mm) beyond each end of the tube. Push the excess stocking into the tube. Fold each end under about 1/2 inch and stitch closed.

🦌 Tack the ends of the three tubes together on one end and then stitch them securely together. Tightly braid the tubes as far down as you can and then tack the ends together. Attach the braid to the barrette by turning the stitched ends of the braid under and tacking each end to the barrette. Adjust the braid and tack it to the barrette along the body of the braid.

Yo-Yo Refrigerator Magnets

Materials

Scraps of fabric about 6 inches (15 cm) square

Small scraps of felt, ribbon, bells, sequins, beads, etc

Magnet tape or magnets from the hem of an old shower curtain

Craft glue

Circle pattern traced from the lid of a 4-inch (10 cm) diameter can or cup

Instructions

🦌 Trace a circle shape onto the fabric squares and cut them out. Sew close to the folded edge of the circle using simple up/down stitches, folding down a 1/4-inch (6 mm) hem as your go. When you arrive at your starting point, tightly gather up the stitches and securely knot your thread. Finger-press the gathered circle flat.

🦌 Glue a magnet or 1-1/2-inch (4 cm) length of magnet tape to the flat side of the circle. Decorate the front (the gathered side) as though it were a wreath or ornament, using the small holly leaf pattern or your own design.

Victorian Enchantments

*V*ictorian colors offer all the glitz of traditional Christmas colors, plus an opportunity to use a new palette of colors and fabrics. Velvets, satins, lamés, and many other fun fabrics are perfectly suited to Victorian-styled projects, and since you'll only need small scraps, you'll get all the thrill of working with these special fabrics without high expenses. Keep in mind that trims such as gold chains, braids, laces, and pearls complement these fabrics well.

The fabric candies make a versatile decoration: display them grouped on a doily-covered plate, as tree ornaments, or tucked into bow loops on a special gift package. The sconces will also inspire you with their decorative potential: hang them on a wall, display them in a flower vase, or slide them between the branches of your Christmas tree. The sconces can be filled with holiday candies, dried or silk flowers, or a handful of tinsel and some small glass ornaments. Although the candies and sconces were made in pinks and mauves to match the pillow, traditional red and green colors would work just as well.

Bonbons

Materials

Scraps of translucent lamé fabric

Squares of satin fabric, at least 12 x 12 inches (30 x 30 cm)

Satin roses, cording scraps, and beads

Gold thread

Cardboard scraps

Glue gun

Tacky glue

Stuffing material (batting, old stockings, etc.)

Doily

Foil baking cups

Instructions

🦌 First decide which shapes of bonbons you'd like to make. *For the square candies,* cut out the satin fabric according to the pattern on page 110. Sew four side seams. Cut a cardboard bottom a little smaller than the top size and glue a small amount of stuffing on top of the cardboard bottom. Place the sewn shape over the cardboard and fold the ends around the bottom of the cardboard. Hot-glue and slip stitch in place. Secure loose ends on the bottom by gluing a length of cording around the bottom. Finish by gluing beads or sequins to the top.

🦌 *For the round candies,* cut out a circle for the top and a long piece for the circular side. With right sides together, sew the side to the top. Slip stitch the ends together. Glue a piece of stuffing to a cardboard bottom and secure it inside the satin shape with hot glue. Glue cording around the bottom sides and finish by gluing a rosebud to the top.

🦌 *For the candy with tied ends,* first glue a piece of satin around a ball of stuffing, slip stitching the ends if necessary. Cut a 6-x 6-inch (15 x 15 cm) square of lamé and machine-hem two facing sides. Wrap the lamé around the ball and tie the ends together with gold thread. Tame any protruding edges with a glue gun.

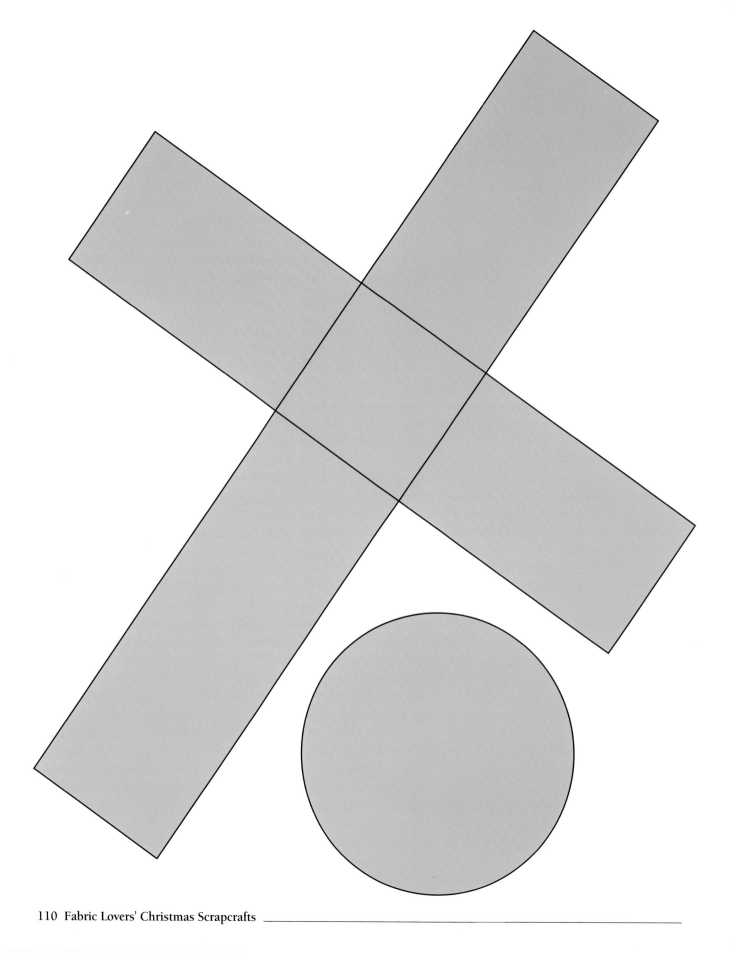

Braided Napkin Ring or Candle Holder Cover

Materials

*3 scraps of fabric, each cut to 3 x 15 inches
(7 x 39 cm)*
Old stockings, hip and toe portions removed
Safety pin

Instructions

🦌 Fold each piece of fabric in half lengthwise with right sides together and stitch along the long ends to form a tube. Turn the tubes right sides out. Attach a safety pin to one end of the stocking leg and use the pin to pull the stocking through the fabric tube. Do not stretch the stocking unless you want a bunched-up effect.

🦌 Trim the protruding length of stocking about 1/2 inch (13 mm) beyond each end of the tube. Push the excess stocking into the tube. Fold each end under about 1/2 inch and stitch closed.

🦌 Tack the ends of the three tubes together on one end and then securely stitch them together. Tightly braid the tubes as far down as possible and then tack the ends together. Fit the braid around a folded napkin or candle holder and mark for length. Sew the ends together to form a ring.

Victorian Sconces

Materials

   Thick drawing paper
   Fabric scraps (satins and velvets work best)
   Lace scraps (optional)
   Craft pearls and rhinestones
   All-purpose glue
   Dimensional fabric paint in a color to match fabric
   By-the-yard craft pearls and satin cording
   Dried or silk flowers
   Gold thread

Instructions

🦌 Experiment with rolling a piece of drawing paper into a sconce shape until you like the result. Unfold the paper and lay it flat. Begin gluing fabric scraps to the paper, keeping in mind where the fabric will overlap.

🦌 Layer on additional fabric scraps (including laces) if desired. Roll the fabric-covered paper into a sconce shape again and glue in place. Allow the sconce to completely dry and then decorate with pearls, cording, rhinestones, and dimensional paint. Last, make a small hole in the top back and make a hanger with gold thread. Fill with dried or silk flowers, candy, or small tree ornaments and some tinsel.

Tip: Create a set of ornaments to match your Victorian fabric crafts by rolling foam balls in glitter and then decorating with satin roses, beads, pearls, sequins, small silk flower buds, charms, and ribbons.

Crazy Quilt Holiday Pillow

Materials

Scraps of velvets, lamés, satins, and laces
    in compatible colors
Square of velvet for pillow back
Approximately 1 yard (.9 m) of satin for ruffle
Tasseled cording
Charms
Decorative threads
Polyester stuffing
Iron-on webbing
1 yard of heavy white cotton fabric

Instructions

🦌 Cut the velvet and white cotton into a square that's just a little larger than you'd like your finished pillow to be. Put the velvet aside. Cut your scrap fabrics into interesting sizes and shapes and attach a piece of iron-on webbing to the back of each. Iron the pieces onto the white cotton square.

🦌 Satin stitch around all the raw edges with different colors of thread. Zig-zag over the satin stitching in a contrasting color. Stitch the tasseled cording over part of the pillow.

🦌 To make the ruffle, measure the outside edges of the pillow and cut a length of 6-inch wide (15 cm) fabric that's twice this length. With right sides together, sew the fabric lengthwise into a tube. Turn right sides out, press, and slip stitch the ends closed. Make a row of gathering stitches, gather the ruffle to fit the pillow, and baste it to the pillow back. Place the front and back of the pillow right sides together and sew all around, leaving an opening large enough for turning. Turn right sides out and slip stitch the opening closed. Finish by sewing charms to the pillow front.

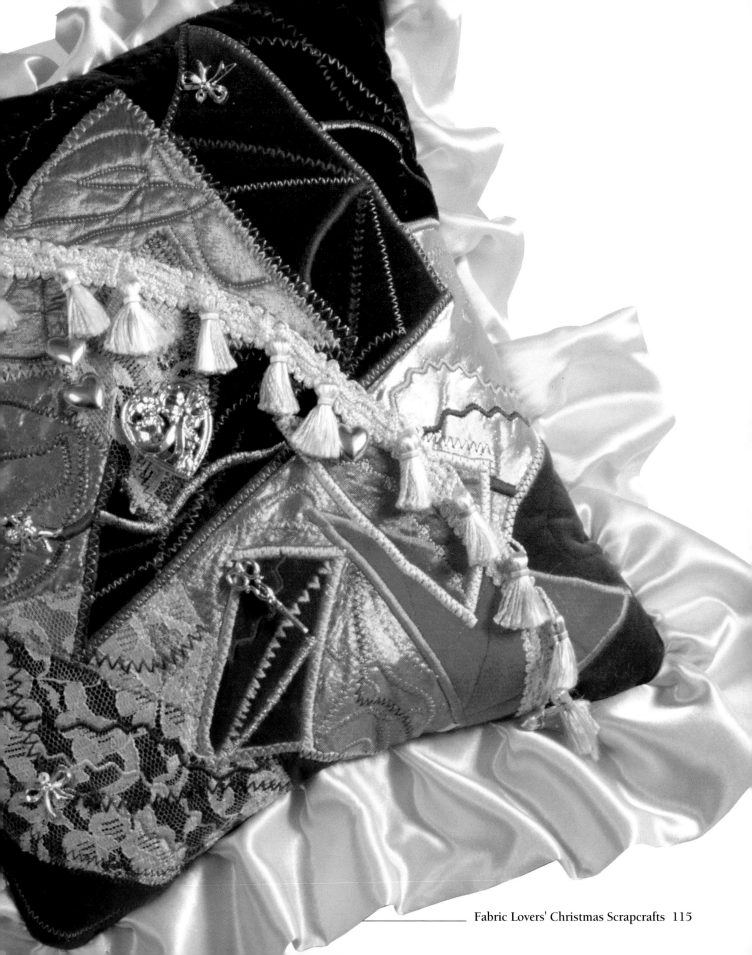

Delectable Confections

*C*onvincing children that Christmas is more about giving than receiving is a difficult — if not impossible — task. Involving youngsters in holiday preparations, though, can help divert their attention from the presents they can't wait to consume to that special excitement that comes from making something with your own hands. Most of the projects in this chapter were designed with the interests and capabilities of children in mind, although they may need a little help from a caring adult.

The sugarplum apron is simple to make from scratch; or, if you're in a rush, you can embellish a ready-made apron with the fabric lollipops and candies. The fabric pencil holder makes a nice holiday knickknack to decorate shelves, and you can use the same basic directions to make a large fabric pot to display poinsettias. The gingerbread house makes a fun kitchen decoration, and the ornaments offer some new ideas for people who've become bored with the same old type of tree decorations.

Sugarplum Apron

Materials

1 yard (.9 m) fabric
Scraps of fabric in several colors to form
the lollipops and hard candies
Stuffing material
Scraps of ribbon in several colors
Double-fold, wide bias binding

Instructions

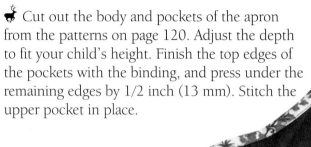 Cut out the body and pockets of the apron from the patterns on page 120. Adjust the depth to fit your child's height. Finish the top edges of the pockets with the binding, and press under the remaining edges by 1/2 inch (13 mm). Stitch the upper pocket in place.

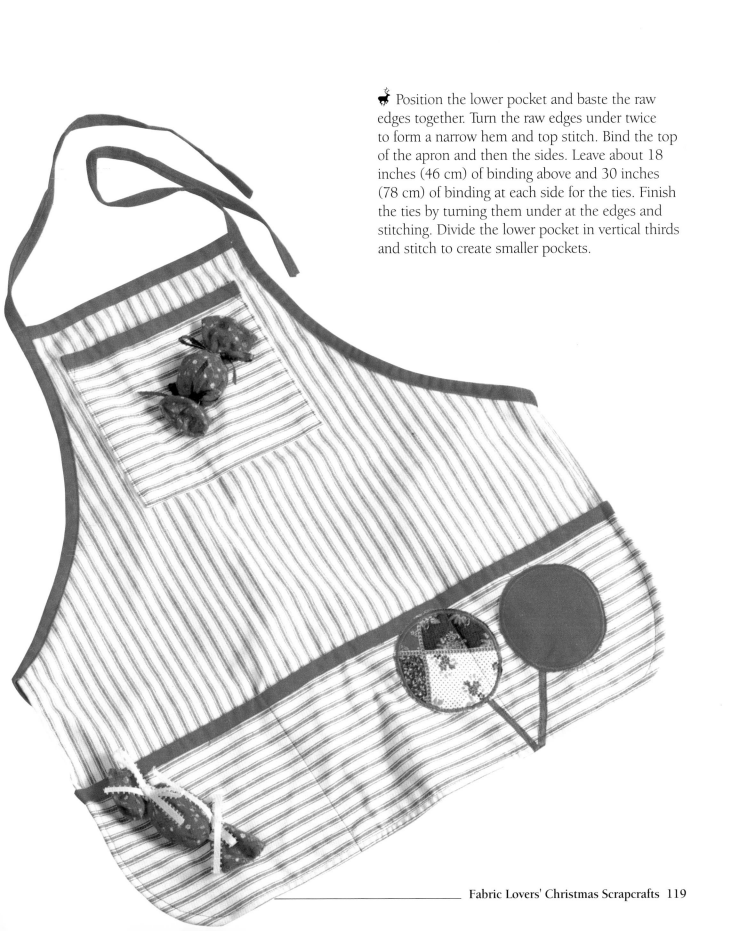

Position the lower pocket and baste the raw edges together. Turn the raw edges under twice to form a narrow hem and top stitch. Bind the top of the apron and then the sides. Leave about 18 inches (46 cm) of binding above and 30 inches (78 cm) of binding at each side for the ties. Finish the ties by turning them under at the edges and stitching. Divide the lower pocket in vertical thirds and stitch to create smaller pockets.

🦌 To make each piece of candy, cut out a 6- x 7-1/2-inch (15 x 18 cm) rectangle. Hem the ends of each rectangle and then sew the side seams with right sides together to form a tube. Turn right sides out and stuff the center. Tie a piece of 8-inch (20 cm) ribbon in a half knot on each side of the stuffing to form a candy ball. Attach each piece of candy to the apron by zigzagging over the knots to secure, and finish by tying both ribbons in a bow.

🦌 To make each lollipop, cut out a circle from a 5- x 5-inch square (12 x 12 cm) and appliqué it to the apron. Finish with a wide machine satin stitch, and then sew a 4-inch (10 cm) length of ribbon in place to form the lollipop's stick. You can decorate the apron with as few or as many lollipops and candies as you like.

Enlarge pattern 320% on a photocopier.

Fabric Canister

Materials

Metal juice can
Scrap of holiday fabric
Scrap of batting
Scrap of green or red felt
Craft glue

Instructions

❦ Measure your can and add 1 inch (2-1/2 cm) to the height and 1/2 inch (13 mm) to the distance around the can. Cut out the fabric and batting to these measurements, taking care that any patterns in the fabric will be square with the container.

❦ Cover the can with a layer of craft glue and press the batting into the glue. Wrap the fabric around the batting, and glue the bottom edge to the batting. Then fold down the top edge by 1/4 inch (6 mm), allow it to overlap the bottom edge, and glue in place. Allow to dry completely.

❦ Trim the batting flush with the top and bottom of the can. Fold the excess fabric over the edges and glue in place. Trace the shape of the can's bottom onto a piece of the felt with a pen and cut out. Trim the circle by about 1/8 inch (3 mm) all the way around and glue it to the bottom of the can. Cut a second piece of felt that is the same length as the fabric you cut earlier, but 1-1/4 inches (3 cm) shorter in height. Position the felt inside the can and glue in place.

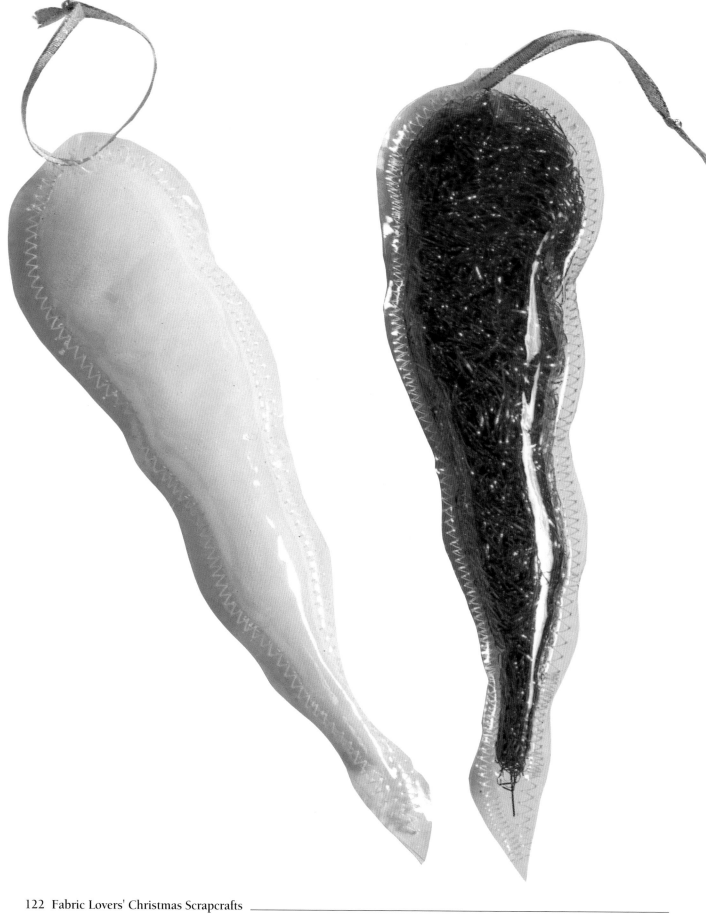

Icicle Ornaments

Materials

Scraps of clear, thin vinyl or translucent fabric
Tinsel or tulle for stuffing
Hole puncher
Metallic thread

Instructions

Cut out two icicle shapes and top stitch them together with a zig-zag stitch, leaving a small opening at the top for stuffing as indicated on the pattern. Stuff the icicle with tinsel or tulle, and top stitch the opening closed. Punch a hole in the top of the ornament and form a hanger with a piece of metallic thread.

Scrap Fabric Ornaments

Materials for Each Ornament

Plastic ornament ball that snaps apart in the center
Scraps of colorful, iridescent fabrics

Instructions

🦌 Cut the fabrics into small squares. Unsnap the
plastic ornament and fill the bottom with tightly
packed fabric squares. Snap on the top and gently
shake the ball to fluff up the fabric.

Gingerbread House

Materials

Scraps of holiday fabric
Scraps of holiday trims
Rectangular food box, top removed
Scraps of cardboard
Craft Glue

Instructions

🦌 Cover the sides and bottom of the box with a background fabric using craft glue. Cut two pieces of cardboard to fit the top of the house. Cover them with fabric and then glue them in place to form the room. Embellish the house with windows, a door, and confections.

Custom Mailbox

Materials

*20- x 23-inch (50 x 57 cm) rectangle of background
    fabric**
1/2 yard (.5 m) iron-on webbing
20- x 23-inch rectangle of lining*
20- x 23-inch rectangle of batting*
1/4 yard (.2 m) red striped fabric
1/4 yard green holiday fabric
1/4 yard red holiday fabric
Freezer paper
Gold metallic thread
Gold braid
Nylon quilting thread
Bias strips in contrasting color
3/4 yard elastic, 1/4 inch (6 mm) wide

Instructions

🦌 Cut the background fabric to a rectangle
measuring 20 x 23 inches. (*Note: This size will
fit a standard mailbox that's 19 inches long and
22 inches across. If your mailbox is a different size,
adjust the size of the rectangle accordingly.) Press
the iron-on webbing to the backs of the red stripe,
green print, and red print fabrics according to the
manufacturer's instructions. Cut out the pieces
according to the cutting instructions.

🦌 Peel off the iron-on webbing from the motifs.
Arrange the motifs on the background fabric as
shown in the illustration and iron them in place.
Press the shiny side of the freezer paper to the
wrong side of the background fabric to create
a better appliqué surface. Zigzag or satin stitch
around the motifs with the gold thread, and sew
two lengths of gold braid to each bell.

🦌 Make a sandwich with the background fabric,
the batting, and the lining fabric, and baste the
three layers together. Machine or hand quilt, and
bind the edges. Cut four 6-inch (15 cm) lengths
of elastic and space them evenly over the 19-inch
side. Use pins or Velcro to attach the elastic to the
other side.

Cutting Instructions

🦌 Cut out two candy canes from the red striped
fabric from the pattern on page 20; turn the pattern over and cut out two more. Cut out three
bells from the green print fabric from the pattern
on page 17. Cut out three bows and three ties
from the red print fabric; turn the tie pattern
over and cut out three more.

Scrap Fabric Basket

Materials

Basket
*Approximately 60 scraps of fabric, each cut to 5 x 5
    inches (13 x 13 cm)*
Tacky glue
Floral wire

Instructions

Create a bow with each square of fabric by making
small pleats in their centers and securing with a
small piece of floral wire. Trim off the wire ends.

Apply a generous coat of glue to the handle, rim,
and sides of the basket. Position the bows in place
around the basket, taking care to distribute them in
an attractive manner. Allow the glue to completely
dry before handling the basket.

Door Knob Decoration

Materials

7-1/2- x 24-inch (18 x 60 cm) piece of holiday fabric
Gold braid
1/4-inch (6 mm) elastic
Narrow ribbon
Jingle bells

Instructions

🦌 Sew the braid to the right side of one of the 24-inch edges, 1-1/4 inches (3 cm) from the edge. Fold the fabric in half lengthwise with right sides together and sew a 1/4-inch seam. Turn right sides out and press. Make an elastic casing by sewing 5/16-inch (9 mm) in from the fold on the long edge. Insert the elastic into the casing and gather to 9-1/4 inches (22 cm). Sew the short ends together, right sides facing. Trim with braid, streamers, bells, and a bow.

Napkin Rings

Materials

Strip of stencil plastic, 1-1/4 x 8 inches (3 x 20 cm)
Strip of holiday fabric, 2-1/4 x 8 inches (5 x 20 cm)
Strip of felt, 1 x 7 inches (2-1/2 x 18 cm)
Craft glue
Scraps of ribbon and beads

Instructions

🦌 Curve the vinyl into a ring and tape it in place. Fold one end of the fabric strip under 1/4 inch (6 mm). Center the fabric on the outside of the ring and glue it in place, folding the edges under on each side. Glue the felt to the inside of the ring to cover the raw edges. Decorate the outside of the ring with scraps of ribbon, beads, and other holiday trims.

Bibliography

Malone, Maggie. Quilting Techniques and Patterns for Machine Stitching. New York: Sterling Publishing Co., 1985.

McCall's Needlework and Crafts. Christmas Crafts. New York: Sedgewood Press, 1984.

Index

A
Album cover, 93
Aprons, 70, 71, 118-120

B
Barrette, 104
Baskets, 6, 7, 69
Bonbons, fabric, 109, 110

C
Canister, fabric, 121
Cards, 58, 59, 84, 85
Casserole carriers, 102, 103
Chair cushions, 40, 41

D
Designers, contributing, 6
Door knob cover, 8
Dress, child's, 44, 45

F
Frames, 88, 89

G
Gingerbread house, 125

L
Lights, felt, 48, 49

M
Magnets, 105
Mailboxes, 5, 52-54

N
Napkin rings, 9, 82, 83, 111, 112

O
Ornaments, 16-22, 32, 33, 122-124

P
Pillows, 72, 114, 115
Place mats, 96-101
Poinsettias, 12, 13
Potholders, 66-68
Pouches, hanging, 14

R
Rug, Santa, 78-80

S
Sconces, 113, 114
Spool Santa, 81
Stockings, 50, 51, 90-92
Success tips, 9
Sweater, 23
Sweatshirts, 26, 27

T
Tablecloth, 73-75
Table runner, 38, 39, 96-101
Tree, fabric, 86, 87
Tree skirts, 30, 55-58

V
Valances, 21, 96-101

W
Wall hanging, 60-63
Wreaths, 42, 43